Research-Based Planning for Public Libraries

Research-Based Planning for Public Libraries

Increasing Relevance in the Digital Age

Joseph R. Matthews

LIBRARIES UNLIMITED

AN IMPRINT OF ABC-CLIO, LLC
Santa Barbara, California • Denver, Colorado • Oxford, England

Library of Congress Cataloging-in-Publication Data

Matthews, Joseph R.
 Research-based planning for public libraries : increasing relevance in the digital age / Joseph R. Matthews.
  pages cm
 Includes bibliographical references.
 ISBN 978-1-61069-007-2 (pbk.) — ISBN 978-1-61069-008-9 (ebook) (print)
 1. Public libraries—Planning. 2. Public libraries—Evaluation. 3. Public libraries—Collection development. 4. Libraries—Special collections—Electronic information resources. 5. Electronic information resources—Management. 6. Public libraries—Aims and objectives. 7. Libraries and community. 8. Libraries and the Internet.
I. Title.
 Z678.M37 2013
 027.4—dc23   2013028319

ISBN: 978-1-61069-007-2
EISBN: 978-1-61069-008-9

17 16 15 14 13   1 2 3 4 5

This book is also available on the World Wide Web as an eBook.
Visit www.abc-clio.com for details.

Libraries Unlimited
An Imprint of ABC-CLIO, LLC

ABC-CLIO, LLC
130 Cremona Drive, P.O. Box 1911
Santa Barbara, California 93116-1911

This book is printed on acid-free paper ∞

Manufactured in the United States of America

This book is dedicated to:

Anna Joy Melchor   *Madison Faith Matthews*
Sam Edward Melchor   *Maisey Hope Matthews*

—the four greatest grandkids in the whole world.

Apa Joe

Contents

Preface

Where It All Went Wrong[*]

Nathan Torkington

Bill Gates wrote a bestseller in 1995. He was on a roll: Microsoft Windows had finally crushed its old foe the Macintosh computer from Apple Microsoft that was minting money hand over fist, and he was hugely respected in the industry he had helped start. He roped in other big brains from Microsoft to write a book to answer the question, "What next?" *The Road Ahead* talked about the implications of everyone having a computer and how they would use the great Information Superhighway that was going to happen.

The World Wide Web appears in the index to *The Road Ahead* precisely four times. Bill Gates didn't think the Internet would be big. The Information Superhighway of Gates's fantasies would have more structure than the Internet, be better controlled than the Internet, and in short it would be more the sort of thing that a company like Microsoft would make.

Bill Gates and Microsoft were caught flat footed by the take-up of the Internet. They had built an incredibly profitable and strong company, which treated computers as disconnected islands: Microsoft software ran on the computers but didn't help connect them. Gates and Microsoft soon realized the Internet was here to stay and rushed to fix Windows to deal with it, but they never made up for that initial wrong-footing.

At least part of the reason for this was because they had this fantastic cash cow in Windows, the island software. They were victims of what Clayton Christenson calls the Innovator's Dilemma: they couldn't think past their own successes to build the next big thing, the thing that'd eat their lunch. They still haven't got there: Bing, their rival to Google, has eaten $5.5B since 2009 and it isn't profitable yet.

I'm telling you this because libraries are like Microsoft.

At one point you had a critical role: you were one of the few places to conduct research. When academics and the public needed to do research into

---

[*] The Text of a Speech delivered to the National and State Librarians of Australasia on 3 November 2011, as Provocation for a Day of Strategic Planning and Forethought Most Profound. Released under a Creative Commons Attribution Share-Alike License http://creativecommons.org/licenses/by-sa/2.5/

the documentary record, they'd come to you. As you now know, that monopoly has been broken.

The Internet, led by Google, is the start and end of most people's research. It's good enough to meet their needs, which is great news for the casual researcher but bad news for you.

Now they don't think of you at all.

Oh yes, I know all of the reasons why the web and Google are no replacement for a healthy research library. I know the critical importance of documentary heritage. But it's not me you're talking to at budget time. It's the public, through the politicians.

They love public libraries, in our country at least. Every time a council tries to institute borrowing fees or close libraries, they get shot down. But someone tries, at least once a year. And England is a cautionary tale that even public libraries aren't safe.

You need to be useful as well as important. Being useful helps you to be important. You need a story they can understand about why you're funded.

Oh, I know, you have *thought* about digital a lot. You've got digitisation projects. You're aggregating metadata. You're offering AnyQuestions–type services where people can email a librarian.

But these are bolt-ons. You've added digital after the fact. You probably have special digital groups, probably (hopefully) made up of younger people than the usual library employee.

Congratulations, you just reproduced Microsoft's strategy: let's build a few digital bolt-ons for our existing products. Then let's have some advance R&D (research and development) guys working on the future while the rest of us get on with it. But think about that for a second. What are the rest of us working on, if those young kids are working on the future? Ah, it must be the past.

So what you've effectively done is double-down on the past.

I like to think of libraries as services in three areas: collections, discovery, and delivery. You maintain big piles of stuff, you help people find the right stuff, and then you let them use it.

In the paper world, this was dominated by the challenges of collection and discovery. So librarians have incredible expertise in preserving words on reeds, on calf skins, on pulped trees. There's huge mana in having a big collection. Collections must grow, they must be complete, deaccessioning breaks hearts and causes shouting matches. And, despite paper, you've been eager innovators and adopters of new information technology: card catalogs and the Dewey Decimal System were profession-changing inventions in their day.

Collections, discovery, and delivery. Delivery is the runt of the litter in the paper world, I'm afraid.

One copy? One precious copy? Okay, sonny, you sit here. We'll bring it here. Don't cough, don't breathe, warn us before you blink. Or, in the old days, help yourself and we'll trust you as a gentleman to bring it back. It was even less successful than pursed lips and the tyranny of the reading room.

The first movie was a camera pointed at a play. They didn't know the possibilities of the old medium, so they reproduced the old structures in the new medium. When confronted with digital technology, you've basically reproduced the old power structures in the digital world.

You want a massive digital collection: SCAN THE STACKS! Give it to Google! Give it to a commercial partner! Just get the damn things digitized so we have a lot of bits of our atoms!

You agonize over digital metadata and the purity thereof. You maybe reluctantly part with your metadata (but not your precious collections!) to Trove.

And you offer crap access.

If I ask you to talk about your collections, I know that you will glow as you describe the amazing treasures you have. When you go for money for digitization projects, you talk up the incredible cultural value. ANZAC![1] Constitution! Treaties! Development of a nation!

But then if I look at the results of those digitization projects, I find the shittiest Web sites on the planet. It's like a gallery spent all its money buying art and then just stuck the paintings in supermarket bags and leaned them against the wall.

You're in the digital world. Bits don't work like atoms. I'll give you five critical ways that bits don't work like atoms.

First, bits are cheap to copy.

By all means protect the digital master, but copies can be plentiful or even ubiquitous.

Physical access has been limited because you have one copy of each physical item, you need to maintain control of that copy to preserve it for the next patron, and copies are expensive to make. Digital copies are free to make, they're nondestructive, they free you from the burden of control, and you can have as many as you want. Those are vastly different rules.

This is, of course, why copyright is such a bugger in the digital age. It's riddled with assumptions about the difficulty of copying atoms that aren't true of bits.

Second, access is expected.

You can argue until you're blue in the face about the intrinsic value of collections, but as your research monopoly has been destroyed, you need to start delivering some other value. Access to those precious collections is it. Collections, discovery, distribution.

If nobody uses your digital collections, what's the point? If nobody can find the digital objects, what's the point? If you recreate medieval standards of access in the digital age, what's the point? You won't get to the 21st century by doubling down on the 11th century.

Your new reading room is your patron's web browser. Are you designing distribution for that? How much did you spend building a new reading room, Bill? How much are you spending on digital delivery?

The first place they start looking for things is Google. Are you designing discovery for that? Do you know how to be found?

Example: the British Library had a company digitise and got limited access and rights to the digitised content. Google contracts have restrictions on your use of the scanned material, too. Is this kind of arrangement acceptable?

It depends on whether libraries are primarily collections or whether you have high expectations for access, too. If you don't value distribution, you'll think these are good choices. The British Library says, "Hey, the physical objects were only available on our premises; this gives more access than there was before. Most importantly, though, we solved the digitisation problem!"

You can see the mistake they made. They focused on collecting digital assets and digitising their physical ones, probably even convened conferences on digital metadata.

And then they hid their fabulous collections out of sight. It's like they WANT to be irrelevant. "Please, don't be one of the first places people visit to research the nation's cultural identity! Let's make it hard for you to do scholarship!"

So, once again: distribution is critical in the digital age.

Third, the Internet is bigger than you are.

In the past, you had knowledge, frozen in books. Ordinary people came to you to get that knowledge. There was a bit of a class divide: those who Create Knowledge and those who Consume it.

Those days are gone. Online, everyone's a creator. Those of you doing digital harvest of Web sites know this. "Look at all the crap we have to save!" (The same is true of legal deposit collections).

The point is that you're saving the stuff that future generations will care about. And, increasingly, the stuff that future generations will care about is online. That's why the Library of Congress acquired an historical and ongoing archive of tweets. Not because a tweet is comparable to a first folio, but because it's what future generations will care about when it comes time to determine the mood of the nation.

I personally believe that the greatest role you play is around the documentary national identity. People come to you to find out about their ancestors, to find out what life was like, to critically evaluate and understand the past.

If you consider your future in terms of documentary national identity, you might do other things. There's a software project here called Kete, Maori for basket, which is a way to capture and preserve family histories, stories of the area, photos, interviews, etc. Imagine a future where citizens contribute to and search these, perhaps through their local public libraries. Wikipedia won't take this stuff, it's not notable, but it's exactly your business: we'll take it and help other people search it.

You might do what the National Library of New Zealand did and dispatch a photographer to Christchurch to document the earthquake aftermath and recovery to ensure adequate documentary record was available to future researchers.

So, in short, much of the nation's cultural life is now happening out there. You need to find more ways to gather it in.

Fourth, bits are so cheap we have too many of them.

Our grandparents grew up with very little. They valued every possession. I know this because I live in my grandparents' old house and I'm still finding balls of oddlengthed twine in the basement. In fact, we humans evolved with very little. We were always starving for food, short of objects, desperate for information.

Now we have too much of everything. Cheap plastic crap from China means everyone can have a crappy version of everything they need. Cheap industrial crap food means everyone can get calories, even though they might not be good for us. And easy copying of bits mean we have too many of the damn things.

Computer scientists think they can solve this problem. We've got indexes and search engines. What we can't programme is critical thinking in humans. That's where librarians come in.

Let's assume that Google's search engine is the state of the art at finding gemstones buried in dungheaps. This state of the art is not great. It struggles with relevance, it tries to filter out spam, and it personalizes so I see different results than you do. And, of course, it's beholden to its advertisers. This can never be the only answer to helping citizens find what they need.

The best solution is when both man and machine work together: librarians make sense of indexes, this is what they do. Computers are great at building indexes. Don't think either-or, think **and**.

Part of a national or state's library's role is to get stuck into this and help. Teach information literacy. Teach basic research skills. Work with schools so kids know how and where librarians exist.

Discovery is important online, and it's not just having accurate metadata and Google.

Fifth, the Internet connects things.

I know, it sounds obvious, but that's what it does. Good broadband is coming to all of us, thanks to the national broadband projects, which are by now too big to fail. Broadband isn't just for sending digitized books across. It's also the medium by which librarians and libraries can work together.

Oh sure, you can share collections. This is threatening to institutions because the collection forms a key part of the institution's identity. Both countries have projects to provide a one-stop-shop search across all cultural collections (search but not delivery!) so we're starting to get our heads around sharing collections. I imagine a National Digital Library where the collections are shared like this. But not just the collections.

You can share services too. You've probably experimented with online services. New Zealand has AnyQuestions, for example. High-quality video conferencing, email, and the Web are ways to deliver human services across the Internet.

If you have people delivering services online (answering questions, making recommendations, entering data, etc.) then you can share people without having to physically move them around. What opportunities does this open up? Share staff between institutions, or have specialist staff offer services in a physical location where they cannot be.

The Internet also connects computers. This is the age of "the cloud." Can you provide equipment for other institutions to use? The National Library has a project to provide regional libraries with an affordable functional modern catalog system so they don't need to spend the dollars themselves. What joint purchasing can you share in this fashion?

So, to recap:

- be useful as well as important
- collections, discovery, distribution
- bits are cheap to copy
- access is expected
- the Internet is bigger than you are
- we have too many bits
- the Internet connects things

You can't afford to be bad at digital. I tell businesspeople: It's your inventory, it's your storefront, it's your customer service line, it's your supply chain, it's your advertising, it's your profit and loss.

For libraries, the Internet is your collection, it's your reading room, it's your catalog, it's your interloan, it's your helpdesk, it's your opportunity to reclaim relevance.

And I'm afraid to say, you're the pointy end of the digital redefinition of culture and heritage institutions and public services, because text is small and the first to go digital. E-books? Next are e-music, e-movies, e-ephemera, e-maps, e-paintings, e-sculpture, and who knows what e-lse. Every archiving institution will face your problems, some are already grappling with them (e.g., the Powerhouse Museum).

Online search? Online helpdesk? Online loans? Every public-facing organisation will face your problems. At least you can take comfort from the fact that you won't be the only ones disrupted by this change.

Finally, let's consider Microsoft. Nobody wants to be in their place: 15 years after discovering the Internet, they're still tipping money into it with little success.

The company that successfully transitioned from a Microsoft business to the Internet age was Apple. When Jobs returned in the late 90s, he threw out the 40-odd products they had and said, "We're going to make computers that are built to connect to the Internet, and the software on them will be Internet-aware software." They focused on four Internet computers (that's where the i in i-Mac came from) and from that success he was able to focus on successful further extensions like iPods and iPhones and iPads.

You need to focus. Success for you is relevance. Make things that people use. Value the skills that your people have and the services they deliver, but don't be a slave to atoms. Value helping people.

Then when someone asks, "Why do we tip all these millions into this?" or "Doesn't Google do that already?" your relevance is your answer. You must do this. Libraries are the homes of critical thought, of long-term cultural preservation, and of democratic access to knowledge. This can't end with the Internet.

Note

1. ANZAC Day is a national day of remembrance in Australia and New Zealand that broadly commemorates all who served and died in all wars, conflicts, and peacekeeping operations.

Introduction

> *We tend to overestimate the effect of a technology in*
> *the short run*
> *And underestimate the effect in the long run.*
> —Amara's Law

Public libraries are indeed living in "interesting times" as we move from an age dominated by physical objects to an age that is increasingly digital. And while the speed of conversion is occurring much faster in the academic environment, public libraries are under increasing pressure to provide an ever-expanding range of content and services in the digital world. Some professional librarians have likened our age as one that is evolutionary while others are insisting that our age is actually revolutionary. Unfortunately, the only way we will be able to tell is that at some point in the future we can look back and decide whether it was evolution or revolution.

As can be seen in Figure I.1, many information resources can be quite easily found, as there are numerous copies available while other resources are

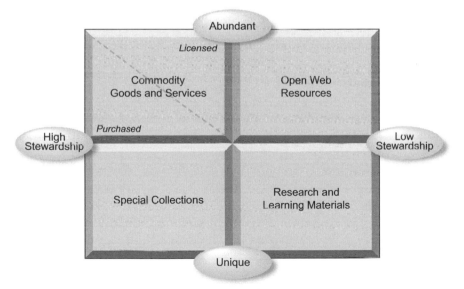

Figure I.1. The Information Resources Matrix. Adapted from The Collection Grid, developed by Lorcan Dempsey and Eric Childress, see Lorcan Dempsey's blog: http://orweblog.oclc.org/archives/001897.html

unique and scarce in nature. Similarly, information resources may require little in the way of stewardship while other resources, typically fragile or scarce in nature, require more stewardship and perseveration.

The whole wide world of information resources (known as the World Wide Web) that are available to anyone, anytime, are to be found in the upper right-hand quadrant of our diagram—Web pages, Twitter streams, blogs, and so forth. And the lower right-hand quadrant provides access to research and learning materials, often found in learning management systems. While traditionally academic institutions develop the materials in this quadrant, it is possible for public libraries to create ways in which community members can share their knowledge and expertise with others.

Many public libraries today are experimenting with new ways to connect with and serve their communities. For example, the Westport (CT) Public Library, the Detroit (MI) Public Library, and the Fayetteville Public Library, among others, are creating MakerSpaces, sometimes called Fabrication Laboratory (Fab Lab), that allow library users access to information and technology that stimulates thinking and creativity. The Anythink Libraries in Colorado continue to evolve as they recreate and redefine how library services are delivered. Some libraries such as Howard County's (MD) are involved with collaborative educational programs and have developed "Kindergarten Here We Come." The Douglas County (CO) Public Library have created their own e-publishing platform and are encouraging relationships with traditional and nontraditional publishers to sell eBooks rather than license them to the library. It is this book's contention that such efforts are vital to the public library's future.

In the upper left quadrant are the materials that libraries have traditionally purchased and increasingly are leasing. In the lower left quadrant are the special collections, rare books, manuscripts, and other unique materials.

Traditionally local libraries have focused their acquisition efforts in the upper left quadrant. However, cooperative efforts and the realities of competition are enabling libraries to redirect resources toward other areas.

How to Use this Book

The focus of this book is on the evolving nature of the collection in a public library. Libraries need to be aware of the wealth of options that are available now or will likely be available in the near-term future that impact how traditional library customers make decisions to use the library (its collections and services) or choose some other option. Whether a library board member, director, library manager, or an acquisitions librarian, there is much that is happening in the environment that will encourage you to take a fresh perspective about the type of collections your library should be providing now.

Ideally, the reader of this book would be inclined to read the book from cover to cover starting with the Introduction and proceeding in a systematic manner reading each chapter in succession. Yet, it is clear that nonfiction works, including books about libraries, are rarely read in this fashion. Thus, each chapter in this book has been written so that it can be read on its own—in whole or in part—and the reader should still derive real value. The end of each chapter contains a Summary section, which identifies the important conclusion based on the content discussed in that chapter. In addition, each chapter contains a Take Action section that identifies activities a library can act upon to gather information that will assist the library in becoming more responsive to their customers.

What this Book is Not

This book is not a "how I done it good in my library" type of discussion. Rather, the book presents a wide array of research about the public library and, in particular, about public library collections, with the intent that these research findings should inform librarians as they make decisions about how to reimagine and recreate their public library.

This book does not present a "cookie cutter" approach to changing the public library but rather suggests a number of activities and a marketing approach that asks librarians to use their creativity and knowledge of their local community in order to make changes to the library's collections and services. The intent is to foster deep thinking about the library and its future in the local community.

What's in this Book

As you will see in chapter one, there are a plethora of competing services and technologies that are pulling apart this tightly integrated space, collections, and services that we call the pubic library. Of particular note, the majority of these forces (development and adoption of new technologies, the growing power of social networks, and so forth) pulling at the library is beyond the control of the library. Chapter two discusses the importance of clearly understanding the community and its needs so that the library can more effectively meet the requirements of different market segments. A research-based, marketing approach to thinking about the library and how it can deliver its services is advocated.

The importance of preparing a number of plans, including developing an updated collection development plan, is discussed in chapter three. Flowing from the library's mission, values, and vision statements, the majority of libraries develop a strategic plan and a collection development plan that is aligned with the library's mission and vision. Chapter four provides a more in-depth discussion of the issues surrounding any collection development plan and the need to update this plan given the findings from a wide variety of research studies.

The characteristics of the library's physical collection and what's best for the customer are explored in chapter five. Viewing the library's collection from the perspective of the customer can be an eye-opening experience. Chapter six explores the virtual side of the library service offering including a discussion of the library Web site, the OPAC (Online Public Access Catalog), and eResources.

The important topic of evaluating the collection by identifying what's hot and what's not, identifying gaps, conducting an availability analysis, considering the use of floating collections (for libraries with branch facilities), and the use of eResources is discussed in chapter seven.

Chapter eight explores the options for different types of facilities, design of facilities, and identifies the variety of ways in which a collection can be configured to maximize customer satisfaction. And finally, chapter nine considers the need to evaluate the library, its brand, the range of services offered, and the ways the library is valued by the customer. Determining and communicating the value of the library to a variety of stakeholders is the final topic of consideration.

Libraries may recognize the need to change in an evolution process but the important point to recognize is that the process for change is one that is constantly ongoing and it is not a topic that is only considered every three to five years when the library is engaged in the strategic planning process.

1

It's Going To Be a Wild Ride

Confront the brutal facts (yet never lose faith).
—Jim Collins

They are defending the library as warehouse as opposed to fighting for the future, which is librarian as producer, concierge, connector, teacher and impresario."
—Seth Godin

Libraries Necd to Rethink Their Strategies

A majority of public libraries have an acquisition's policy that is based in the 1950s mentality. Back in the early 1950s, a little more than 10,000 titles were published annually and many libraries bought a majority of these titles. Now, however, the situation has dramatically changed with more than 300,000 print titles published annually and public libraries buying about 20,000 titles. In addition, more than one million self-published eBooks became available in 2012.

In former times, libraries were purchasing a majority of the published books and assisting customers in finding what they wanted. It was relatively easy to discover what was new and coming simply by examining the reviews published in *Library Journal, Publishers Weekly, Choice*, and some other publications. Libraries focused on providing access to the materials patrons already wanted, resulting in libraries ignoring their role in the discovery of new books. Yet, today, faced with the veritable tidal wave of new print and electronic books, libraries are ill-equipped to assist their customer in finding high-quality new materials. Thus, libraries have to radically change the way they support the discovery process of new print books (sometimes called pBooks) and eBooks or people will go elsewhere.

In addition, libraries need to fundamentally reexamine the strategies they use to provide access to materials in a physical facility and their involvement

1

with their community by providing interesting and stimulating meeting places as part of a process to anchor their communities.

Challenges

Today, public libraries confront a plethora of challenges and competition from arenas, some not even visible even five years ago. Among the many of these marketplace forces and trends, many are beyond the library's immediate ability to influence and change. Yet, in order to thrive and remain relevant to those in our communities, public libraries must change, perhaps even faster than we would like.

It is safe to say that libraries came into existence to provide for the afford-able sharing of hard-to-find and expensive books and other materials. The scarcity of materials and information allowed libraries to develop tools whereby they could control (gatekeeping) and organize access to the primarily print-based library collections. In such an environment, the role and responsibilities of the library are clear-cut and unambiguous. Yet, libraries of all types no longer function in a world of information scarcity. Libraries increasingly encounter the perception among some stakeholders that everything is available via the Internet—so why do we need the public library? For the vast majority of organizations, including libraries, the Internet has changed everything! The amount of change and the speed with which change occurs signify that the waves of change are not simply breakers coming ashore at high tide but rather that a series of large tsunamis are moving our way.

Competition and Forces of Change

Among the more important of these challenges that will impact the public library in large and small ways are:

The Internet has changed everything! The number of U.S. households that now have Internet access slightly exceeds 80 percent and two-thirds of our households have broadband access (Rainie 2012). And while a digital divide clearly remains, the divide is shrinking with each passing year. Robert Metcalfe and others have suggested the primary value of the Internet, often called the "network effect," is that as others joined the Internet, it became more useful. Metcalfe has suggested that the value increases not on a linear scale but on an exponential manner.

The amount of information accessible via the Internet has been compared to turning on a faucet the size of several large fire hoses. To take advantage of this flood of information, a number of innovative Internet-based services have been developed and are used by a large number of people worldwide. Perhaps the best-known and most-used services include Google (for searching), Facebook (social communities), eBay and Amazon (purchasing used and new materials), sharing pictures (Flickr), sharing videos (YouTube), and so forth. The Internet has allowed people to move from being consumers to creators of content that is then shared and linked using Twitter, blogs, Facebook, Web sites, and other Internet-based tools.

The distribution and reuse of information digitally via the Internet is rapidly changing the world—as libraries know it—rewarding those who aggregate and scale toward a common infrastructure.

Networked communities. The amount of new content that is created and shared every day is simply staggering. Today, more than 72 hours of videos are uploaded to YouTube every minute (more than double than a year ago). The barriers to sharing artistic expression and individual thoughts have never been so low. The Pew Internet Project has found that while most people do not create new content (most of us lurk in the background), the sheer number of people that are creating new content has the Internet growing at exponential rates—rather than linear rates—as shown in Figure 1.1 (Rainie 2012). The popularity of social media sites, especially Facebook, demonstrate that people enjoy being "connected" with family, friends, and almost friends for all kinds of revealing information.

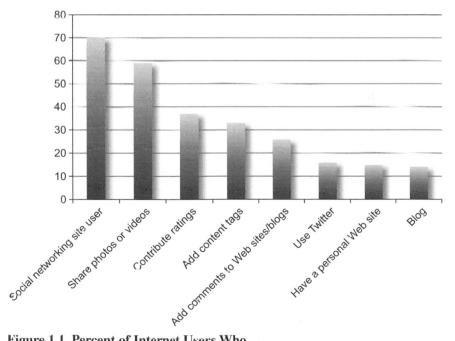

Figure 1.1. Percent of Internet Users Who ...

Discovery happens elsewhere. People discover items of interest using Internet search engines, RSS aggregators, recommendations found on various Web sites, and resource networks created as a result of social network sites. Almost no one will seek out a library Web site to gain access to resources.

Digitisation impacts perceptions. Given the significant financial resources Google has applied to the digitization of books, the speed with which more than 15 million books have been digitized has contributed to the perception that "everything is available on the Web." And Google is still in the process of digitizing even more books. And still other groups are also actively involved in the digitization of books and other materials. Some publishers and database vendors work to make sure that their electronic journal articles are visible in Google Scholar and other discovery tools, which also contributes to the perception that it is not necessary to visit the library (in person or virtually). And some larger libraries have ongoing digitization projects to add even more content to the Web. The implication of this for the public library is quite significant and means that the value of the local collection is being, and will continue to be, marginalized.

The impact of search engines (Google). The reality is that almost any kind of information is immediately accessible using an Internet search engine (in more than 80 percent of the cases this means Google who does more than five billion searches a day). The actuality is that people are more interested in convenience than quality. And people are searching using desktop computers, tablets, smartphones, and other hand-held devices. In short, people want and are demanding immediate access to information.

Purchasing online. People are increasingly turning to the Internet to purchase items, small and large. The range of materials that can be purchased from Amazon alone is quite impressive—not only books but also MP3 tracks, games and software, movies, electronics and computers, garden and tools, groceries, health and beauty, and much, much more. Chris Anderson (2006) has called the ready availability of unique items in a large inventory of items accessible via the Internet the "Long Tail."

Declining perception of value. The stakeholder's and the public's perception of the value of the library as well as the value of professional librarians is almost totally disconnected from reality. Given the Internet's pervasive impact in almost everyone's life (the always on society) and the ability to quickly gain access to a limitless variety of information, people simply do not understand how the public library contributes to the welfare of the community. And while a majority of librarians recognize the sometimes-poor quality of online search results, the reality is that convenience trumps the high-quality collections and services that libraries have historically provided.

We are not in the flow. Increasingly people are organizing their work in network environments and libraries and their resources are not even on the horizon. Thus libraries need to create library services around the workflow of students, entrepreneurs, moms with small children, seniors, and so forth. Software applications demand the ability to interact with other applications—RSS feeds, Web services, apps, and so on.

Providing access to eBooks is problematic. With the variety of eBook readers and the proprietary nature of some eBook formats, it can be difficult for a library customer to download an eBook to their eReader. This means that many popular eBooks are simply not available at the local public library. Libraries are thwarted with their inability to provide a convenient and seamless solution to their customers. Some have suggested that many publishers want to serve their eBook customers directly rather than going through a middleman (this process is disintermediation). Despite the fact that only about 11 percent of the U.S. population has an eBook reader, the demand for eBooks is growing at a significant rate. For example, Amazon sold more eBooks than it did pBooks during 2011.

Access rather than ownership. Many libraries are finding that a larger share of their acquisition's budget is being devoted to licensing electronic content (eBooks, eJournals, and other eResources) rather than purchasing that content. And a fair number of publishers impose price increases each year that greatly exceed the average rate of inflation. This means that the local library is losing more and more control over how they can spend their budget each year.

Information is abundant; attention is scarce. As more and more content proliferates so does the ability for an individual to focus on any one item. Thus, convenience of use becomes extremely important.

Rapid change. The information and communication's technology arena is dynamic with the entry of new startups (and failures) each year due to the rapidly evolving nature of hardware and software technologies. The time intervals in information technology—codex to movable type, to the Internet (digital content), to search engines, to Google's algorithmic relevance ranking, etc.—is happening in shorter and shorter time periods. If you are comfortable using a computer-based software tool, then the tool is probably on its last legs!

People are always on. Given the ubiquitous nature of hand-held mobile devices and the fact that people interact with these devices from the time they first awake till they drop off to sleep each night, people expect information to be delivered anywhere, anytime. Today, there are more mobile phone subscriptions (327 million) than the total U.S. population (315 million). Thus, information content must be able to be "squeezed" so that it can be delivered to a very small hand-held device. Mobile devices are being used as a new means of sustaining, embodying, and creating social networks that bring people together. Dempsey (2009) suggests that mobile devices alter the consumption patterns of individuals in fundamental ways. People connect and share themselves through "social objects" (photos, videos, music, or other objects) and thus become connectors to content for others.

Streaming content. The streaming of videos and movies will replace the use of DVDs in the not-too-distant future. Already, streaming content is responsible for more than half of all Internet traffic.

Cloud computing. Computer technology (servers and associated software and other IT-based infrastructure) can now be based anywhere (it's in the cloud) rather than an organization installing and maintaining systems locally. And cloud-computing-based services are typically much less expensive than attempting to do-it-yourself.

The leaking of digital materials. Digital materials degrade much faster than their print counterparts—digital content held on magnetic materials must be refreshed periodically or the content begins to degrade or become totally lost. The average life span for an Internet site is fewer than 40 days!

The demand for print books is not slacking. With more than one million books being published last year from regular publishers plus a flood of self-published books plus print-on-demand enterprises, the reality is that demand for traditional printed books is not declining. And unfortunately, the public library is buying a smaller percent of the publishing output each year.

Putting data to work. Library data, especially catalog data, is inherently lazy since it is located in a silo and it rarely escapes. We need to identify ways that we can release library data, without compromising patron privacy, so that people will find the library in new and interesting ways.

Media is losing its impact. Large-scale media—for example, newspapers, magazines, commercial television—is losing its audience, and the associated advertising revenue is no longer as powerful as it once was. Many newspapers have ceased publication and many other newspapers and magazines have become slim imitations of what they once used to be.

Economic distress. The worldwide economy is experiencing significant troubles due to the excesses of the housing and Wall Street "bubbles" as well as excessive borrowing at all levels of government. Unemployment continues at high levels and many people will continue to struggle and suffer until the economy eventually rebounds. Given the global recession, the prospects for improved levels of employment is not encouraging. The results of this economic situation for almost all public libraries are reduced or flat-line budgets.

Changing demographics. The population in the U.S. is changing and in some communities the changes are quite dramatic and noticeable. The population is getting older; Hispanic populations, including many Spanish-speakers, are growing; and people continue their migration from rural to urban centers.

Infrastructure. High transaction costs have led to the locally assembled library collections yet, in the last decade or so, reduced transaction costs have resulted in distributing activities across the Internet. The result is that libraries are redundantly managing local infrastructure, which creates little distinctive value. Users are to be found at the network level and less frequently at the local library.

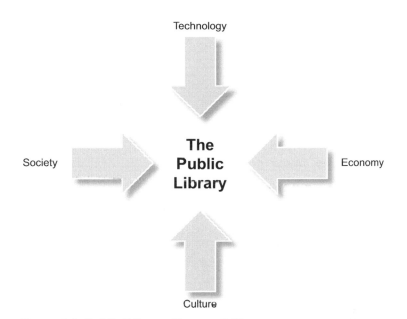

Figure 1.2. Public Library Forces of Change

Library space is being repurposed. Libraries are moving portions of their collections out of the building to make room for new, and more flexible, space. There is pressure to provide more computers so that more people can simultaneously gain access to the Internet. Demands for other types of space within the library are also growing.

All of these forces of change—technology, culture, society, and the economy—are illustrated in Figure 1.2. For many, these forces of change are already being felt and it seems that the tsunamis of change are occurring with some regularity rather than a once-in-a-lifetime occurrence.

> *Status quo thinking is a race to the bottom.*
> —John Bellina

Summary of Findings

Given all of these forces of change, it is clear that the public library needs to embrace some amount of change. Each library needs to answer two very important questions: How much change? And, what kind of change? If the public library wants to remain a vital part of its community and play a role in the lives of its customers, then understanding those customers and their needs is pivotal. It is also clear, without too much thinking, that all library customers do not visit the library, whether physically or virtually, with the same needs or set of expectations. Thus, the library must figure out what are the different community segments, sometimes called market segments, that exist within its community. This focus on the customer and their unique needs is what this book is all about.

2

Understanding Your Market

One of the most important tasks of the marketing function in an organization is to identify the most appropriate ways to divide up their potential audience.—Liz Hall

The joy and fulfillment that public libraries around the world bring to people is an incalculable benefit that, if it could be measured, would assist libraries in communicating their true impact in the lives of individuals and in the community itself. Imagine a camera at the door of the library that would capture the smiles of people as they were leaving. A whole series of photos could be displayed and as one was added one could drop off the large screen(s).

The challenge for those who are involved in developing and providing services to library customers, in meeting and exceeding customer expectations while at the same time providing transparency and accountability, is real. Part of the challenge is gaining an understanding of the community and its characteristics so that the library can provide the collections and services that appeal to the library's customers. This description of responding to the needs of the community is another way of saying that the library has embraced customer-focused marketing principles.

Introduction to Marketing

Some believe that marketing is all about getting people to suspend their rationality for a period of time so that someone can sell them a product or service (that they probably don't need). In reality, marketing is all about identifying, serving, and satisfying human needs. Effective marketing requires a customer or consumer orientation rather than a product or service orientation. Alternatively, effective marketing has an outward orientation (toward the customer) rather than an inward orientation (toward the product or service).

> *Marketing begins and ends and begins again*
> *with understanding what patrons need.*
> —Jill Stover

Librarians often make the assumption that they know the needs of their customers. Yet, there is substantial evidence of a disconnect between the perceptions of librarians and the views of ordinary customers. For example:

- Several *Public Library Effectiveness Studies* were conducted and survey respondents from seven different constituency groups were asked to rank order the factors that they considered important to library effectiveness. Studies were conducted in the U.S. (Childers and Van House 1989), Canada (Mittermeyer 1999), and New Zealand (Cullen and Calvert 1993; Calvert and Cullen 1994). Each of the studies achieved remarkably similar results. It is significant that the two groups farthest apart in terms of their perceptions were library customers and public service librarians. The most important factors for library customers were: convenience of hours, range of materials, range of services, staff helpfulness, and materials quality.

- *Starting a Search.* Many libraries contend that they are in the information business. These libraries are, of course, ignoring that Google has, in fact, already won the "information war"—more than five billion searches a day. According to the OCLC *Perceptions* report, 82 percent of respondents start their information searching using a search engine (read Google!) while a miniscule 1 percent start with the library's Web site (De Rosa et al. 2005). And by 2010, use of search engines to start their information search had increased slightly (84 percent) and "not a single survey respondent began their information search on a library Web site" (OCLC 2010). The convenience of the search engine trumps the quality of resources available at the library. And the OCLC survey respondents favor libraries for free Internet access, free materials, and special programs. The same respondents favor bookstores for coffee shops, current materials, and meeting their friends.

- *Information Source of Last Resort.* A survey of business people found that when they are looking for information that the local public library is almost at the bottom of the list. The library comes *after* customers, suppliers, friends, associates, relatives, newspapers, magazines, trade publications, consultants, lawyers, accountants, trade associations, and banks (Vaughan et al. 1996). Yet another study found that people with an information need consulted a public library only 17 percent of the time (Chen and Hernon 1980). People were more likely to consult with other people or institutions and that the public library was near the bottom of the list.

- *Not Finding What You Want.* Most librarians would suggest that their library provides items that are useful for their patrons. Yet, a plethora of availability studies consistently suggest that the customer will likely find a specific title of interest on the library shelf only about 50 to 60 percent of the time (see chapter eight in Matthews 2007). Given this "half right" success rate, it is not surprising that some customers find the public library experience frustrating.

> *The aim of marketing is to know and understand the customer so well the product so well the product or service fits him and sells itself.*
> —Peter Drucker

For a large proportion of the community, the public library is not even on the radar screen. A marketing-oriented approach to identifying the needs of different customer segments and then exceeding the expectations of each customer will do much to ensure that the library becomes more relevant in the lives of those who live or work in a community.

Libraries, like other nonprofit organizations, vary in their awareness and use of marketing principles. This is really surprising since many marketing principles are embodied in age-old library activities such as publicity, public relations, advertising, and extension (outreach) services.

Marketing, which is both a science and an art, is all about exploring, creating, and delivering value to satisfy the needs of a target market (a specific group of customers). While many companies have a marketing department, marketing is, in reality, too important to leave to a single marketing department. Marketing is only effective if the whole organization delivers the promised value and satisfies the customer.

Understanding Your Community

While the airline industry has not yet recognized this particular reality (one size seat for all in economy class), we do not live in a one-size-fits-all world. Library customers, like customers everywhere, come in all shapes and sizes with different needs and expectations of the public library. Understanding the needs of different groups of customers is called market segmentation. Market segmentation identifies the salient characteristics among different groups of people and uses these distinctions as the basis for differentiated marketing activities such as promotions, communications, advertising, and so forth.

It is possible to examine possible public library market segments from three perspectives:

- Demographics
- Use
- Market Segmentation
- Benefit Segmentation

Demographics

Demographics partially predict who will use the library and who will not. Other non-demographic factors such as lifestyle, social roles, and travel distance also heavily influence library use.

Public libraries have historically identified market segments by age—preschool, elementary school students, teens, families with small children, seniors, and so forth. Once identified, libraries have developed a series of services that will appeal to each market segment. For example, story time programs for preschool children, Mommy-and-Me story times, and so forth.

A combination of demographic factors is more important than a single characteristic. The characteristics of the public library user that have been discussed and analyzed in a large number of user studies include (Powell 1988):

- **Education**. The more education an individual receives the more likely they are to use the public library. Education is the single most important predictor of library use and it is not unusual for more than half of library users to have some college, a college degree, or even some postgraduate work. While it is true that income, occupation, and education are all inter-correlated, regression analysis demonstrates that everything disappears except education.

- **Age**. Consistent evidence suggests that those who use the library the most are young adults and that use of the library declines with age. However, Kronus noted that the relationship between public library use and age was misleading and not statistically valid. According to an ALA survey, the distribution of public library users are shown in Figure 2.1 (ALA 2002):

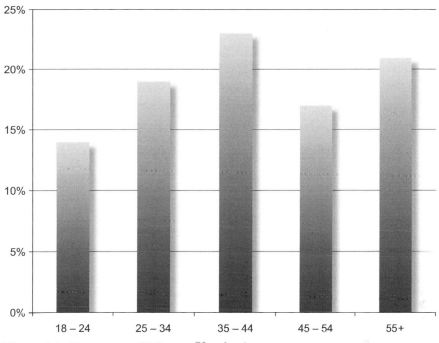

Figure 2.1. Frequency of Library Use, by Age

- **Number of Small Children**. Adults with small children are more likely to have a library card and to visit the library on a fairly regular basis (the greater the number of children the more frequently the library is used). Households with children are much more likely to use the public library than those without children—61 percent compared to 35 percent (Lynch 1997).

- **Family Income**. Individuals with higher incomes will use the local library more frequently. However, use is greater among middle-income levels than among the poor or the rich. It may be that low use of the library by the poor is related to poor reading skills or the fact the lower income households have considerable fewer books than their more affluent counterparts. A 1991 survey showed that use of the public library was clearly correlated with family income (Scheppke 1994). With increased income comes discretionary time for reading and information-seeking activities.

One study found that higher incomes tended to be associated with higher library usage rates per capita using a "library activity" index composed on circulation, in-library use of materials, number of reference transactions, and annual program attendance (Kopczynski and Lombardo 1999). This study also noted that other factors affect the use of library services including the availability and location of branch libraries, number of hours open, size and scope of the library's collection, and so forth.

- **Sex**. Women are more prone to use the library than men although several authors have noted that men use reference services more frequently while women use circulation services more. While women use the library more than men, taking employment status into consideration and holding education constant, the dominant use by women disappears.

- **Marital Status**. Single individuals use the library more than married people with no children. This is likely the case since single adults are younger than married adults and use declines with age. In addition, married adults probably have less leisure time than single adults due to domestic responsibilities.

- **Ethnicity**. Depending upon the ethnic population within a community, use of the library will generally reflect the relative proportions of the population, although more use will likely occur among members of the white ethnic group. One national survey found that 56 percent of users were white while 38 and 42 percent of the respondents were Hispanic and black respectively (Scheppke 1994). Another more recent national survey found that among households that had used a public library, 80 percent were white, 9 percent black, and 7 percent Hispanic, which is roughly representative of the distribution of the U.S. population (Lynch 1997).

Another study found that patrons of color use the library for educational support and for information gathering more than do their Caucasian counterparts (D'Elia, and Rodger 1994).

Racial and ethnic minority groups are growing at a much faster pace than the general U.S. population. Thus, a public library should periodically review the demographic shifts that are occurring within its geographic and service area boundaries and adjust its services accordingly.

Using a geographic information system, or GIS, Christine Koontz (2001, 1992) mapped demographic and library use data for several public libraries with branches and found that branch libraries serving primarily minority populations had higher in-library use, higher reference transactions, and greater program attendance, while at the same time having lower circulation figures. This is significant since most public library systems will often use circulation as the sole indicator of a branch library's performance.

As the demographics of many communities continue to change, that is traditional minority groups are growing numerically and in political power. As such, some public libraries will need to assess whether their traditional library services, provided in the majority of branch libraries, are the right mix of services for this underserved population.

Use of the Library

Among the many published and the many more unpublished reports prepared by library staff and consultants, several consistent public library user characteristics emerge. The characteristics most frequently examined in these studies include: sex, age, education, family income, marital status, and the number of small children living at home.

Kronus (1973) prepared an analysis that determined what variables explained some part of the use of the public library. Her analysis suggested that education, urban residence, and family life cycle factors predicted the rate of library use. The commonly used factors of age, sex, and race had no independent influence on library use.

Attempting to better understand the relationships between library use and user characteristics, George D'Elia (1980) developed a model with a hierarchy of variables that included such items as individual characteristics, patron awareness of library services, perceived accessibility, and ease of library use. He concluded that users of the public library perceived the library as more accessible than nonusers and that frequency and intensity of use were related to awareness of the range of available library services.

Ronald Powell (1984), looking for a more predictive answer concerning library use, examined the personality of the user. He found no link between personality type and use of the library.

A second approach is to analyze the population by use, which results in the often referred to split of users and non-users. Using the report capabilities of the library's automated system, it is possible to sort the registered borrowers into several groups:

- **Customers**, sometimes called patrons or users, are registered individuals with a library card. These individuals can be subdivided into three broad groups:

  ○ *Frequent customers* are those who use the library on a monthly or more frequent basis. Research suggests that in general about 80 percent of a library's circulation can be accounted for by 20 percent of the library's customers (the actual percentages may be slightly off in some libraries). The 80/20 rule in a library setting was first noticed by Richard Trueswell and has also been called the Pareto effect. Joseph Juran called this effect the "vital few and the trivial many."

○ *Moderate customers* are those who use the library bimonthly or less frequently.

○ *Infrequent customers* are those who have used the library sometime during the past year.

• **"Lost customers"** are individuals who visited the library, completed an application form, and received a library card. However, they have not used the library in the past year. Thus, while they "found" the library at one time, they are now "lost."

One of the real limitations of a library's integrated library system is that it does not help the library keep track of other uses of the library—attending programs, reading newspapers and magazines, using Wi-Fi, and so forth. This is a challenge that the vendors must start addressing soon. And libraries must get creative in tracking such usage in meaningful ways.

Almost all organizations that spend any money on marketing knows that it is easier to attract "lost" customers than it is a non-customer—often by a factor of 50. The costs to attract a "lost customer" to return to the library are considerably less than trying to attract non-users who have never visited the library before. Given that the library has contact information for their lost customers (name, address, telephone number, and, in most cases, an email address) it is quite simply amazing that libraries do not use this information to communicate on a regular basis about what is "new" about the library. Attractive and regular emails could be sent to these lost customers to encourage them to find their way back to the library (providing the "lost customers" are given the opportunity to stop receiving emails from the library).

It is true that many individuals refuse to provide their email addresses due to privacy concerns. The library must persuade the customer of the benefits of potential future contacts and then live up to those expectations. The customer should be able to establish different levels of contact—overdue notices only, new materials alerts, forthcoming programs, and so forth.

A recent analysis of library customer satisfaction survey data revealed that it takes as many as 20 visits to the library before an individual develops the library "habit" and becomes a consistent customer (Matthews 2008).

- **Non-Users** are people within a community who may or may not be aware of the location of the library and the range of services that they offer. Joan Frye Williams has called non-users "civilians." Note that these civilians can be divided into two groups: those who can be enticed to the library and those who will never, under any circumstances, use the library.

In addition to *use value*, economists have come to realize that people can derive satisfaction (and value) from the mere existence of a public good such as the public library. In addition to *non-use value*, the literature has called this concept by a number of other names—bequest value, existence value, prestige value, vicarious consumption value, education value, and option value.

The public library's non-use value can be considered as the utility that people obtain from a library other than through its active use. This non-use value can be divided into two categories:

1. An option for an individual to use the library at some time in the future. The library is valued and prized as an institution that enhances the quality of life.

2. An option for others to use the library now and in the future. Individuals may be willing to support the library for the benefit of others.

Altruistic motivations (that is, concerns that those that are less fortunate such as poor people, street people, people of color, and others, should have equal access to the totality of services offered by the public library) will be taken into consideration when people are asked to reflect on the value of a public library.

Not surprisingly, challenges arise when attempting to quantify the value of non-use benefits as estimated values are most often based on a number of assumptions and estimates. In addition, some individuals simply are not active readers and do not even consider use of the library. Some people, called alliterates by G. K. Beers (2010), can read but they choose not to do so. The three groups of alliterates include:

1. *Dormant readers*—People who do not find the time to read but who like to read

2. *Uncommitted readers*—People who do not like to read but indicate they may read sometime in the future

3. *Unmotivated readers*—People who do not like to read and are unlikely to change their minds

High Involvement	Use of electronic resources Use of librarian-mediate reference Interlibrary loans
Medium Involvement	Use of reference collection Borrowing of books and other media Photocopying
Low Involvement	Program attendance Browsing magazines & newspapers Use facilities for personal study

Figure 2.2. User Involvement with Library Services

One study in a public library setting found that lost users and non-users alike did not use the library due to distance, inconvenience of hours, and their preference to purchase their own materials. Further analysis revealed that adding to the collection in each location would entice lost customers to return while building more locations and adding more hours would attract nonusers to the library (Sone 1988).

Another way to visualize use of the library is to conceptualize the level of customer involvement in library services as shown in Figure 2.2. Low-involvement services depend on the facilities available and on individuals who typically serve themselves. And a customer that only uses the library's electronic resources would be another example of a low-involvement customer. Medium-involvement customers are those who use the collections intensively but typically have little or no interaction with library staff members. High-involvement customers are those who have a high degree of interaction with librarians, collections, and the facilities.

A survey of 661 public library customers in Taiwan found that about 77 percent of the customers were low-involvement, 20 percent as medium-involvement, and only 3 percent were high-involvement (Chang and Hsieh 1997). An analysis of customer satisfaction found that high-involvement customers focused on staff empathy, medium-involvement customers were interested in the availability of materials, while low-involvement customers were interested in the amenities of the physical space.

Frequency of Visits. Depending upon the community and characteristics of its population, public library users visited the library (ALA 2002):

- Weekly   14%
- Twice a month   11%
- Monthly   9%
- Less than once a month   31%

A U.S. News/CNN poll (1995) found that 67 percent of adults went to a library at least once in the past year. And a 1996 survey conducted by the U.S. Department of Education found that 44 percent of individuals had used the library in the last month and a total of 65 percent had used the public library in the prior year (Collins and Chandler 1997). And a more recent national survey found that 46 percent used a public library within the last six months and that a total of 57 percent had visited the library in the last year (Vavrek 2000).

Summarizing the results of a number of users studies it is possible to note that on average, 20 percent of the adults use the public library at least once a month. Thus, a fairly small proportion of users will account for most of the visits to the library. This statistical phenomenon is known as the normal Pareto distribution. That is, a relatively small number of users (20 percent) will account for 80 percent of the visits to the library. This same Pareto principal will also apply to circulation of library materials.

Location of the User. The vast majority of people visiting a public library, especially a branch library, live within a few miles of the library facility. Christine Koontz (1997), summarizing the research in this area, noted that some 57 percent of users lived within two miles; 27 percent live within two to four miles; and 5 percent live within five miles of a public library.

In general, library usage falls off rapidly with distance, although urban residents who wish to walk to their local library prefer smaller libraries (Palmer 1981). And since library facilities typically are designed to last 25 years or longer, locating a facility in other than the "best" site will result in lack of access and reduced use, which means diminished efficiency and effectiveness. In a study that examined demographic, spatial, quality of the library, and library use variables, Christine Koontz (1992) found that demographic variables alone do not accurately predict library use, but that typographical features, hours of operation, size of the building, and unique population characteristics will affect library use. In short, the factors that matter to the location of fire stations, retail stores, and other important facilities where time to travel to a specific location is important are also essential, or should be key to libraries. However, once people have developed the library "habit," they will travel farther in order to obtain more or better materials (Welch and Donohue 1994).

When putting together a marketing plan for your library, perhaps one of the most effective first steps is to prepare an analysis of those who already possess a library card. The analysis can calculate the cardholders by age, gender, zip codes, census tracks, married adults (with and without children), and so forth. Sometimes the results will reveal surprises! The Columbus Metropolitan Library combined their patron registration data with a commercial market segmentation database in order to segment customers into some interesting groups (Circle and Bierman 2009). These groups include:

- *Power users*—those individuals who checkout the majority of items (remember the 80/20 rule), place holds, and are active in browsing the collection.

- *Bookworms*—tend to check out a large number of items each visit and make frequent (often daily) visits to the library.

- *Media hounds*—primarily borrow CDs and DVDs.

- *Socialites*—use the library to meet with others while only slightly borrowing materials. Others use the computers and no other library services.

The library might need to conduct a survey to learn about its online users. In many communities the user of the library's Web site is younger than the average library customer.

Market Segmentation

Market segmentation combines traditional demographic data with lifestyle and consumer buying behaviors. Thus market segmentation categorizes households along several dimensions, including income, household type, age, ethnicity, education, employment, housing type (single-family homes, apartments, mobile homes), and preferences, such as leisure activities and media preferences. With market segmentation, a public library can track, by customer library use, data in order to plan marketing campaigns, develop new services, target support for election campaigns, build customer loyalty programs, identify new patrons, increase library use by existing patrons, site new facilities, and build public awareness.

Several libraries, including the Topeka and Shawnee County (KS) Public Library and the Suffolk County (NY) Cooperative Library System, have used a market segmentation system developed by CIVICTechnologies (Futterman and Michaelson 2012; Millsap 2011). Using patron registration data from the integrated library system (ILS), each address is geocoded so that a variety of maps can be produced. In addition, data about item type, material type, collection code, plus the location used to borrow the materials, is also noted. The individual transaction data is then aggregated to better understand how each market segmentation type currently uses (or does not use) the library. This then allows the library to better understand who their customers are as well as developing a clear picture of the market potential in the library's service area. The goal is to develop strategies that will help the library reach several goals:

- Increase existing customers' usage

- Increase customers' satisfaction

- Reach out to the unserved.

In the end, planning is all about connecting with people and building relationships based on actual knowledge about the needs of various market segments.

Benefit Segmentation

A more recent approach in the library environment is to use benefit segmentation, which is to identify market segments by causal factors rather than descriptive ones. That is, the benefits sought by users of the library will shape their behavior much more accurately than other approaches to market segmentation (Haley 1968). It is important to understand that more frequent or heavy users of the public library will have different needs and benefit expectations than infrequent library users. Thus it would seem important to understand the benefits that different groups of library users are searching for.

Acknowledged experts on users and how they use libraries, Brenda Dervin, and Benson Fraser (1985), documented 16 benefits or "helps" by tracking what people did with information and attempting to determine the "end result." They felt that information was a "means to an end" and that a better understanding of the transition of means to ends would be helpful as libraries planned for the future. Among their "helps" were:

- Found direction/reached goals/got skills

- Felt connected

- Got ideas/understanding

- Got happiness/pleasure

- Got support/emotional control

Dervin and Fraser noted that people who visited public libraries were significantly more likely to experience "happiness/pleasure" than those that visited other types of libraries. A nationwide survey discovered that public libraries had a positive impact on the quality of life (51 percent) and improved the lives of the respondents (41 percent) (Vavrek 2000). Of those that felt that the local library had improved their lives, a large majority felt that the library provided educational enrichment, improved their reading skills, or provided entertainment.

In a study of Pennsylvania public libraries, McClure and Bertot (1998) found that libraries play an important role in the everyday lives of people. Their report is filled with anecdotes that illustrate the qualitative impact that public libraries play. A similar study in England found that: public libraries support education, careers, job training, and literacy; libraries are a cohesive force within a community by supporting special groups, e.g., seniors; and foster community pride (Usherwood and Linley 1999).

Table 2.1. Reason for Use of American Public Libraries

Rank	Reason	% of visits for
1	Borrow books	67
2	Use reference materials	47
3	Consult the librarian	47
4	Read newspapers or magazines	31
5	Connect to the Internet/email	26
6	Take out CDs, videos or computer software	25
7	Hear a speaker, see a movie, attend a special event	14

The 2002 ALA survey found that adults go to the local public library for a number of reasons as shown in Table 2.1. If the survey had included both children and adults, the results would likely be different.

When people use the Internet, some 65 percent do so "for enjoyment or hobbies," 57 percent to "get information for personal use," 53 percent "for a school assignment," 35 percent "for a work assignment or to keep up to date at work," and 27 percent "to help find a job" (Vavrek 2000). A more recent study (Dutton and Blank 2011) found that employed individuals tend to use the Internet more than students and retired individuals. Internet usage focused on travel plans, information about local events, news, health information, sports information, and finally job-related information.

> *Public librarians must stop confusing the most commonly occurring activity in the public library (leisure reading) with the most important activity of the public library (lifelong learning). Counts and accountability are not synonymous.*
> —Kenneth Shearer

For libraries that are interested in adopting an outside-in perspective in order to better understand customers and their needs, it might be more fruitful to understand what benefits customers receive from a physical or virtual visit to the library. That is, the package of likely benefits that result from use of the library will be different for each market segment of the population. The primary advantage of segmentation includes:

- A better understanding of customers and their needs
- A more effective targeting of resources

The market segments would be defined by the primary use of the library rather than relying on demographic information. A pilot study at the Dover (DE) Public Library resulted in identifying eight identity-related reasons for a visit to the library (Institute for Learning Innovation 2005). These reasons included:

- **Experience Seeker** looks to the library as a venue for entertainment or social connection. They like being around people and may be seeking an activity to occupy their time. (Selected by 36 percent of the respondents.)
- **Explorer** is an individual that is curious and loves to learn but does not have a specific topic or subject agenda prior to the visit. (Selected by 35 percent.)
- **Problem Solver** has a specific question or problem they want to solve. They might be looking for health information, investment information, planning a trip, and so forth. (Selected by 23 percent.)
- **Facilitator** is an individual who is there to support someone else in their use of the library—their children or a friend. (Selected by 16 percent.)
- **Patron** is an individual with a strong sense of belonging to the library. They belong to the friends group and will often volunteer for the library. (Selected by 16 percent.)
- **Scholar** is someone with a deep interest and a history of research work in one topic area such as genealogy or religion. (Selected by 9 percent.)
- **Spiritual Pilgrim** is someone who will focus on the library as a place of reflection or rejuvenation. (Selected by 8 percent.)
- **Hobbyist** is an individual looking to further their interest in a particular interest area. (Selected by 4 percent.)
- **Other** includes those individuals who do not fit into one of the above groups—they are there to drop something off or pick up something. In some communities, this would include the homeless who are looking for a place to hang out and perhaps use email.

In Singapore, the data collected from a survey of the country's population was subjected to a cluster analysis and seven segments with distinct learning and reading-related lifestyles were identified (Keng et al. 2003). These lifestyles included:

- **The career minded** hold strong beliefs regarding education and family and turn to the library first for their reading.

- **The active information seekers** possess a moderate education and have an entrepreneurial spirit and place greater importance on social status and material well-being.

- **The self-supplier** prefers to purchase their own books, is better educated, and holds managerial or executive positions.

- **The group readers** have an avid appetite for reading and are heavy library users.

- **The narrowly focused learner** consists of students who read to fulfill a course requirement.

- **The low motivator** possess little interest in reading.

- **The facilitators** are females with lower education levels and value highly the importance of the library for their children.

As shown in Figure 2.3, the identification of the reasons for possible use of the library leads to insights about reading habits and visits to the library.

The benefit segmentation approach has the possibility of significantly improving library services. How would (could) a library organize its services (other than they are currently organized) to better meet the needs of each benefit segment group?

The answer lies in developing a clear picture of each customer group based on benefit segmentation rather than social-economic characteristics so that the library better understands their needs and how the library can add value. Rather than considering the value proposition from a broad perspective, it is better to try to understand why different benefit segment groups value and use the library. So the question becomes: "What is your library's unique value proposition for each group?" Why does each group use the library rather than going to a bookstore, spending time online seeking information from a search engine, and so on?

Another related technique that can be used either separately or in conjunction with benefit segmentation groups is to develop personas. A persona is a hypothetical representation of a natural grouping of people that drive decision making for a project. While personas are not a real person they do represent real people with unique needs. A persona focuses on what is valuable to that group and their goals when they visit a library. Personas provide a means to understand both existing customers and noncustomers' expectations of the library's services and products.

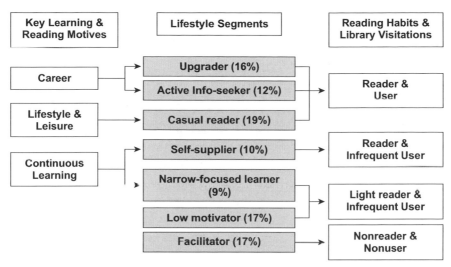

Note: The percentages in parentheses refer to the weighted sample

Figure 2.3. Summary Findings of the Seven Segments

Personas are developed not by using customer surveys but rather by involving a number of people in talking about various themes and values. These conversations are recorded and subsequently analyzed. In a project funded by SirsiDynix, seven personas were developed in a public library setting. For each of the seven personas, a profile was developed that explored: a typical day at the library, their information-seeking behavior, their ultimate goal, and their frustrations. The seven personas include:

- **Discovery Dan**—who symbolizes the adult non-researcher user
- **Haley High School**—who epitomizes the high school customer
- **Jennifer**—who is representative of the parents of teenagers
- **Mommy Marcie**—who exemplifies the parents of young children
- **Rick Researcher**—who embodies an adult researcher (usually with their own personal computer)
- **Senior Sally**—who characterizes senior citizens, and
- **Tasha Learner**—who symbolizes the adult researcher (without a personal computer).

The consulting firm MAYA Design was part of a team that designed a new library experience for several buildings that were remodeled for the Carnegie Library of Pittsburgh. They observed and interviewed a large group of users and

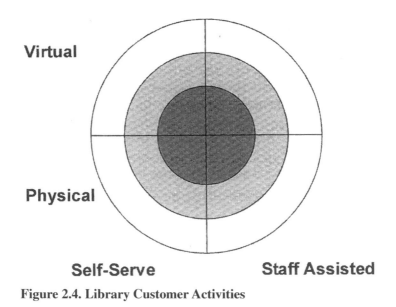

Virtual

Physical

Self-Serve   **Staff Assisted**

Figure 2.4. Library Customer Activities

used eight categories of customers in order to better understand the needs of each group. Their categories include: Non-user, Searcher, Learner, Media guy, Explorer, Teen, Parent, and Senior.

Once the various benefit segments have been identified using interviews as a way to determine why people are using the library, it is possible to conduct a brief survey asking members of each group to rate the importance of various library services and identify the frustrations that they experience when attempting to use the service. The results can then be plotted to show the importance of these services as shown in Figure 2.4. Michael Magoolaghan (2008), a board member of a small public library in Media, Pennsylvania, demonstrates that an information architecture (IA) tool, used in most IA projects can also be applied to a small library.

The inner circle represents the core or most important library functions or activities, from the perspective of the customer. The middle circle represents supporting activities while the outer circle represents the peripheral activities. The core activities might be the selection and borrowing of books, picture books, DVDs, CDs, and attending programs. Supporting activities might be doing research for school or business or our personal lives, and reading magazines or newspapers. Peripheral activities might be to meet friends, surf the Internet—check email, attend meetings, hang out with friends, and so forth.

The frequency with which an activity is mentioned in the survey determines its place within the circles.

What Motivates a Customer?

The decision of an individual to use the public library according to Marchant (1991) occurs when the user's motivation is stronger than the inhibitions that discourage use. Four specific motivators were examined and Marchant found that all four—home and family life, vocational growth, religion, and politics—led to the use of the public library.

A number of studies have consistently found that library use is not related to race (D'Elia et al. 2000, Welch and Donohue 1994). This suggests that demographics alone are not accurate predictors of library use. In reality, library users often possess:

- A desire to explore the world around them

- A desire to use books and other media to assist in their explorations

- Knowledge of libraries and how they are organized.

A study by Madden (1979) found that regular library users actively sought new experiences and consistently worked to improve themselves, their family, careers, hobbies, and the like. Library non-users dislike change, watched television a great deal each week, had few activities outside the home, and were less educated than library users. Other studies (for example, Zweizig 1973) found that the level of community involvement and the desire to influence the world was positively correlated with library use.

Barries that Limit Use

Among the many possible inhibitors of use of the library are: inadequate or inconvenient hours of service, inadequate library collection, inconvenient library location, lack of parking, lack of library skills, competing demands for time during non-work hours of the day, poor health, lack of transportation, and so forth.

Thomas Ballard (1986) in a review of a number of studies found that factors outside the control of the library account for a large percentage of nonuse among community residents. The lack of free time was noted by more than half of the respondents from across the U.S. in another study (D'Elia et al. 2002). Despite the inhibitors, the public library remains a popular destination for a great many individuals within a community.

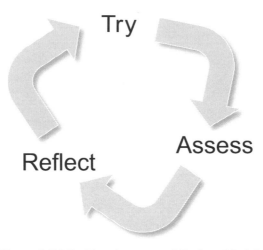

Figure 2.5. The Try, Assess, and Reflect Model

Assessing Your Success

Should you embrace evidence-based librarianship, it is important to recognize that implicit in this approach is the reality you are willing to enthusiastically embrace change. The evidence-based librarianship movement encourages the professional librarian to consider the evidence of what has and has not worked and then begin the process to implementing best practices. Yet, it is also true that the librarian must reflect upon the evidence of how well the change is taking place in your specific library. Thus, as shown in Figure 2.5 a simple three-step process is recommended to guide the change process.

A number of writers have suggested in this time of rapid change it is important to fail quickly. That is, try something, gather some data about the effectiveness of the change, and then make some adjustments. For most libraries, deciding that it is time to update the long-range plan is a time-consuming process that will likely result in few changes to the existing long-range plan. And appointing a committee is another way to stifle innovation.

Try

Using the evidence found in the professional literature, a library might consider changing the way in which a service is delivered, or creating a new service. The decision to try implementing something new obviously will have a greater chance of success if the decision is made within the context of:

- Understanding the needs of the community served by the public library

- Recognizing that the needs of community members will change over time depending upon their demands at any moment in time

- Acknowledging that groups of people with similar needs are customer segments from a marketing perspective

- Identifying the ways an existing service can be improved for a particular market segment by involving individuals from this segment in exploring their needs in greater detail

- Aligning the library's mission and vision with the needs of the community

- Changing the way in which an existing service is delivered, or introducing a new service in the library. For example, the library may wish to implement a merchandising-based approach to the display and storage of materials rather than relying on traditional library shelving.

- The fundamental question to be answered is: What does the library want to achieve? In order to achieve its vision, the library may need to consider entering into partnerships with other organizations within the community.

Assess

After something changes, the library should identify the evaluation and impact (outcomes) questions that should be asked. One of the important issues is to be able to understand how the change impacts the physical or electronic collections provided by the library. Among the areas to be explored are:

- For each market segment, the library should be able to answer two fundamental questions:

  ° What services and how much of each service is used by each market segment?

  ° What difference (impact, benefit) does each library service have in the life of each customer in each market segment?

  ° In addition, to using quantitative data from the library systems, the library should also be able to identify what customers are saying about the library and its services when they use social media (Hernon and Matthews 2011).

- The library may wish to determine on an ongoing-basis the level of customer satisfaction by administering a satisfaction survey. Tracking the results over time will help the library better understand the degree to which it is meeting the needs of each market segment.

- At a broader level, the library may wish to assess the impact the library is having on the societal level.

- When examining the library's internal processes, remember that the library exists in a competitive environment and that the activities that once added value may no longer do so. The library must ensure that its processes are faster, better, and cheaper than they were a year or two ago.

Reflect

The important point to remember is that assessment, sometimes called evaluation, is a process and not a goal. The goal is to improve the quality and relevance of library services to each market segment that have been identified by the library as the target market.

Using all of the data gathered during the assess phase, consider what the data has to say. Should changes be made to a specific service? For example, the library may be tacking what portions of a collection are being used as a result of a program that was recently offered at the library. If the program was focused on creating winning resumes, then the library should be interested in what materials pertaining to resumes were borrowed shortly after the program was completed. Some of the questions that might be addressed include:

- Are there specific formats that are being used less than they should?

- Should some material formats be moved so that they are more visible as the customer enters the library?

- Is signage for specific collections visible from several points within the library?

- Is the evaluation of a service being accomplished using multiple means?

- Does the data suggest an incremental improvement or should the library consider a more radical approach?

- Does the data make sense?

Making a Difference

The OCLC *Perceptions of Libraries* reports (OCLC 2005, 2010) found that public libraries have a single and dominant brand—books. And as even the occasional user of the library knows full well, the public library has always been providing services that range beyond books. Yet, librarians are stuck with the reality that people simply view the library as a warehouse of books! What to do? The answer, in part, lies in an OCLC report, *From Awareness to Funding* (2008). A combination of telephone and an online survey was administered to 1,901 adults in the U.S. The findings from the report suggest that:

- Perceptions of the librarians by the community members influence the degree of library funding support.

- Use of the library is only slightly related to library funding support.

- Library funding supporters more often see the library as "transformational" rather than "informational."

- Targeting marketing messages to the right market segments of the voting public is key to driving increased support for U.S. public libraries.

The report goes on to further to suggest that there is:

a need to appeal to both the heart and mind of the potential voter, positioning the library as an important part of the community's infrastructure that plays a key role in providing equal access to resources vital for thriving in today's digital world. (OCLC , 2008, p. 1–7)

From the customer's perspective, a transformational library:

- Encourages you to be thankful for the beauty in life

- Helps you recognize what you have learned

- Is empowering

- Assists you in finding hope and optimism

- Instills confidence

- Serves a serious purpose.

And since the perceptions of the public librarian have a strong influence on funding support, it suggests that the librarian needs to spend much more time out of the library and in the community. People will recognize if a librarian is passionate about making the library relevant in this period of rapid change. People respond to librarians who are knowledgeable about the needs of the community and focus the library's range of services on meeting those needs. The librarian needs to assist the community to recognize that the public library delivers four essential benefits:

- Equal access for all is perceived to be a fundamental right of American democracy.

- Sharing community values (sharing community assets, respect for community and self-reliance)
- A special third place that has unique and distinct qualities
- Improved community stature as the library is viewed as a symbol of freedom of thought and progress.

The largest investment of value to the customer of the library is being able to access either/both the library's physical or electronic collections. Customers typically come to the library in order to borrow or download a specific title view or some materials that will meet the need of the individual. Others come to participate in program offerings, interact with others for a variety of reasons, work quietly alone, and so forth.

The intent of this book is to demonstrate that the public library provides real value to an individual or to a larger group of individuals that can be categorized as a market segment. Focusing on the changing needs of the various market segments being served by the library will mean that the library will remain relevant in the lives of the community that is being served. For the foreseeable future, a public library's collection is going to remain as the primary generator of value in the minds of its customers and thus the library needs to ensure that this expensive resource is receiving maximum use.

Summary of Findings

As we have seen in this chapter, embracing marketing principles means that the library has a better understanding of the market segments that it is currently serving and those segments that it could do a better job. Having a clear understanding of the needs of each market segment means that the library is better positioned to meet their needs. A library that provides the combination of a recent and relevant collection along with quality services will result in customers who will return again and again.

One of the real ironies of any public library is that when economic conditions force a reduction in the library's budget, the use of the library increases—often dramatically. Marketing can assist the library in assessing and changing the service mix to better meet the needs of the customer in these challenging times.

It is vitally important to realize that data about the community and library customers is gathered and analyzed to drive marketing, services, and programs! What motivates individuals to use the library is that they perceive that each time they visit (physically or virtually) they will receive real value. In short, using the library is worth their time.

Take Action

Your public library should:

- Prepare an analysis of who is using the library's physical collections. Break out the users by a broad range of age and sex and determine the amount of use (borrowing) by material type, by use of the nonfiction collection (using 25 to 40 classification groups), and so forth.

- Compare the demographics of the library users with that of the community as a whole. What segments of the community are not using the library or are not using the library with any degree of regularity?

- Prepare an analysis of those who use the library's Internet workstations. Are they different in any way to those who borrow materials from the library?

- Prepare an analysis of who is using the library's electronic collections. What databases do they use and how many documents and journal articles are downloaded? Break out the Internet users by a broad range of age and sex.

- Think about conducting a series of focus groups to find out what they like about the library and what they do not like. Each focus group should have a specific segment of the community (teens, young adults, parents with young children, seniors, and so forth).

- Consider combining library registration data with a lifestyle database to come up with a more detailed picture of the library customers.

- Think about conducting a survey to find out the reasons why people come to the library. Once the library has prepared an analysis of the survey data, consider how the library could reorganize its services (and collections) to better meet the needs of the library customers.

Developing a Plan

You can never plan the future by the past.
—Edmund Burke

Plans are nothing, planning is everything.
—Dwight D. Eisenhower

The word strategy is military in nature and refers both to an army and to a general or the commander-in-chief who is directing the movements and operations of a campaign (application of military force).

In spite of the military origins, the use of strategies, strategic planning, and strategic management have been successfully applied to all types of for-profit and non-profit organizations, including libraries. The use of strategies and strategic planning fall into four categories:

- A *plan* or a means from getting from here to there.

- A *pattern* of actions over time. For example, focusing on a particular market segment.

- A *position* that reflects decisions to offer products and services in particular markets.

- A *perspective*, vision, or direction of what the organization is to become.

A strategy is an action plan that focuses on how a given objective will be achieved. Strategies are designed to move the library toward the vision of the library and to eliminate the gap that exists between where the library is today and where it wants to be tomorrow. Note, however, that strategies are not programmatic goals and objectives that most libraries develop as a part of their long range planning. Programmatic goals typically are separated into several categories (resources, services, technology, and staff development). Such an approach does not reflect a coherent set of strategies but is rather a potpourri of goals and objectives and represents a strategy known as "unfocused and more of the same."

Ask any group of people to define strategy and the most likely first response will be that strategy is a *plan*, a guide for future action or a means to get from point A to point B (Mintzberg 1987). Thus, in this case, strategy is the "how" the library will act to achieve the intended outcome or destination. However, asking these same individuals to articulate the actual strategy pursued over the past few years by the organizations that they work for will, in some cases, reveal that there is a difference between the written strategies and the actual strategies currently being employed.

Still, other people, most notably Michael Porter who is acknowledged to be one of the world's strategy gurus, consider that a strategy is a *position*—the organization is able to place a specific product or a service in a particular market. These individuals believe that strategy is looking out to the external marketplace. These individuals are looking to see the "big picture."

However, when all of the definitions and perspectives are all boiled down, strategies are really concerned with one fundamental question. Organizational strategies concern "how":

- *how* to grow the organization,

- *how* to satisfy customers,

- *how* to provide services

- *how* to overcome the pressures of competitors,

- *how* to respond to changing market conditions, and

- *how* to manage the library and develop needed organizational capabilities.

The *hows* of strategy tend to be organization specific, customized to meet the organizations situation and objectives.

Think of strategy as a bridge; values are the bedrock on which the piers of the bridge are planted, the near bank is today's reality, the far bank is the vision. Your strategy is the bridge itself.
—Gordon R. Sullivan

In order to develop successful strategies, an organization needs to simultaneously carefully plan and seize upon opportunities, have a broad vision, focus on details, and establish direction from the top and embrace participation from all levels within the organization. Or, as observed by F. Scott Fitzgerald (1936), "The test of a first-rate intelligence is the ability to hold two opposed ideas in the mind at the same time and still retain the ability to function." To successfully consider and implement a series of strategies will mean that a librarian will need to understand, hold, and synthesize such opposing views.

The secret to understanding an organization's plan is to see how the most precious resources within the organization (people's time, money, and other resources) are allocated and used to deliver products and services. Within many organizations, including many libraries, a goal may be articulated but since there is no change in the way resources are applied, staff quickly realize that the goal is not important, and that maintaining the status quo is all that is expected.

The real purpose on any planning process is to identify the library's customers and how the library will provide products and services that will be of value to these customers. The second part of the plan should identify what capabilities the library needs (sometimes these capabilities are called "critical success factors") in order to be successful.

> *The Five Most Important Questions*
> *1. What is our mission?*
> *2. Who is our customer?*
> *3. What does the customer value?*
> *4. What are our results?*
> *5. What is our plan?*
> —Peter Drucker

Setting Direction

The primary role of top management and the library board is to set the direction for the library. This can be best accomplished and communicated to the stakeholders through the development of a strategic plan. Among the topics that should be addressed in such a plan are:

- *Mission.* The raison d'etre for the existence of the library. Why does the library exist? Who does the library serve?

- *Values.* The basic beliefs that the library is founded upon. Values rarely change as they reflect something that is viewed as important or almost sacred.

- *Vision.* Usually prepared by top management with the involvement of many others it focuses on what the library will be like in ten to 20 years (time horizon may vary).

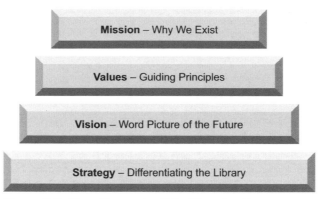

Figure 3.1. Core Concepts of the Planning Process

- *Strategic Focus.* Strategies are the key things that will differentiate the library from its competitors. While many may be involved in the development of the strategies, ultimately top management is responsible for their selection and implementation.

- *Critical Success Factors.* These are the important things that the library must do well to overcome today's problems, assist in meeting and exceeding the competition, and assist the library in achieving its vision.

The above concepts are at the core of an effective library—informing and inspiring all stakeholders, guiding decisions, and aligning the actions of all staff members (see Figure 3.1).

The Mission

Cartoonist Scott Adams (in Line 1996) suggested that:

> The typical mission statement is a long, awkward sentence [paragraph, or page] that demonstrates management's inability to think clearly."

Some organizations call the mission statement their "purpose statement" or the central reason for existing. Whom do you serve? What roles do you play in the lives of your customers? What are you trying to accomplish? The answers to these questions are found in the mission statement.

The organization's mission statement should describe its present activities ("who we are and what do we do"). A good mission statement has a number of characteristics including a focus on the customers served by the library, an indication of the products and services provided, and how the customers benefit.

One research study found that a clear mission statement was one of four primary characteristics of successful non-profit organizations (Knauft et al. 1991). The value of a powerful mission statement is that it can energize employees, reduce the need for supervision, and assist in making decisions within the organization. As David Osborne and Ted Gaebler (1992) noted:

> The experience of hashing out the fundamental purpose of an organization—debating all the different assumptions and views held by its members and agreeing on one basic mission—can be a powerful one. When it is done right, a mission statement can drive an entire organization from top to bottom.

If a library's mission statement not only sets a clear definition of "who we are and what do we do" but also indicates where the organization is headed, then it has combined the concepts of a mission statement and strategic vision or a vision statement into a single statement describing both where it is now and where it is going. However, it is important to distinguish between the library's mission and strategic vision.

> *Some organizations make the mistake of turning their mission statement into "hero sandwiches of good intentions."*
> —Peter Drucker

Drucker (1988), the renowned teacher, author, and consultant, has further noted that purpose and mission are the foundation upon which an organization's plans and strategies are built.

Only a clear definition of the mission and purpose of the business makes possible clear and realistic business objectives. It is the foundation for priorities, strategies, plans, and work assignments. It is the starting point for the design of managerial jobs, and, above all, for the design of managerial structures. Structure follows strategy. Strategy determines what the key activities are in a given business. And strategy requires knowing "what our business is and what it should be."

Clarity of organizational purpose helps the library's top management team become better leaders. Such clarity can assist the organization in understanding what rules help control conflict and which rules may need to be changed. The mission statement can also assist individuals in disconnecting the means from the end so that the discussion is about what problems to solve rather than about solutions. David Osborne and Ted Gaebler suggest that if governments stick to *steering* (purpose and problem definition), then they are less likely to be a captive of any one approach to *rowing* (solutions).

Values

Values are the guiding principles and the deeply ingrained operating rules of an organization. They represent the ways things get done in an organization. These beliefs or enduring principles influence the attitudes and behavior of a library's employees. Exciting and dynamic organizations, including some libraries, have written a value statement that clearly articulates:

- The value of the customer
- The importance of staff members
- How things are accomplished
- The importance of efficiency
- The type of communication that is valued
- And the role of performance measures

Organizational values are deeply held beliefs that are manifested by staff members in their daily activities. These are the principles that guide an organization in its conduct and its relationships. Having a concise and compelling statement of values helps staff understand what they can do to assist the library in achieving its vision.

Having an articulated set of values assists the library in recruiting individuals that have similar values, aid in motivating staff members, support the process of implementing changes within the library, and act as a guide in the event emergencies should arise.

Some of the words articulating an organization's values that occur fairly frequently include: integrity, openness, courtesy, respect, accountability, and responsibility. Clearly the goal is to go beyond a listing of values in order to craft a set of values that are meaningful to the library's staff members and customers.

One of the important challenges facing librarians as they strive to define their values is to recognize the gap that exists between those who see themselves as personal custodians and institutional guardians of received library values and others who believe librarians should be working to create value for library customers. At one end of the spectrum are those who view values as more to comfort, advocate for, and defend libraries rather than embrace values that focus on providing value to customers.

> [Being] valuable is not about our professional values; in the paradigm of the value of . . . libraries we are the producers, not the customers of our services. Our personal sense of what is valuable doesn't matter unless it matches that of our customers. (Rodger 2002)

The Vision

The vision statement sets out long-term targets and success criteria for the library and acts as a focus for identifying the key strategic activities that need to be accomplished if the vision is to be achieved (Olve et al. 1999). A good vision statement is clear, memorable, motivating, customer-related, and its goals or targets can be translated into actions, which can be measured. A vision statement can be thought of as a coherent and powerful statement of what the library can and should be (three-to-five) years hence.

If a vision statement is too long, then it will fail the test of being memorable. An inspiring vision:

- Invigorates and challenges

- Is an important ingredient for change

- Will positively impact on the behaviors of staff members

- Is the standard against which all decisions are made

- Will almost dictate the choice of performance measures that will be used to measure progress

And unless the vision is focused on meeting customer needs, then the reason for the library is being ignored. As Peter Senge (1998) has observed:

> Vision translates mission into truly meaningful intended results—and guides the allocation of time, energy, and resources. In my experience, it is only through a compelling vision that a deep sense of purpose comes alive.

It is imperative to look beyond today and think strategically about the impact of new technologies available now and in the short-term future, how customer needs and expectations are changing, identifying the consequences of engaging or ignoring the realities of competitors, and examining the other external and internal factors that drive what the library needs to be doing to prepare for the future. Armed with a clear and compelling strategic vision, managers and other staff members have a compass to guide resource allocation and a basis for crafting strategy to get the library where it needs to go.

As a part of the process of identifying and creating a vision, consider that a library could be viewed from a number of perspectives. Among the more noteworthy perspectives are:

- *A physical collection.* A collection of materials with a variety of formats—books, journals, audio-visual, microforms, documents, maps, and so forth.

- *Nurturing the independent learner.* Provide support for the independent learner, particularly the individual interested in expanding their horizons.

- *Knowledge navigator.* In addition to providing traditional in-library reference service, the library can also provide an online 24/7-reference service. This can be complemented by providing and updating a variety of pathfinders.

- *Information technology.* The library provides access to information and computer technology as well as staff with superior information management skills.

- *Information provider.* The library provides access to its collection and skilled professional librarians to assist users in meeting their information needs. In some cases, the library focuses on collecting and organizing information about topics that would be of interest to those served by the library.

- *Document deliverer.* Deliver documents, in particular copies of journal articles, using interlibrary loan and links to document delivery firms.

- *Researcher.* A skilled librarian may provide their research skills to customers of the library.

- *Meeting place.* The library provides access to meeting rooms of varying sizes.

- *Information literacy.* Assist in developing information management or information literacy skills.

- *The "preferred" information intermediary* known for providing access to quality information resources (physical and electronic). As the library moves toward providing more electronic resources it becomes more of an "invisible" intermediary, sometimes called a portal.

- *Memory institution.* The role of preserving materials of value to the library's customers may be important for some libraries.

Organizations with winning vision statements are able to express an energizing view of the future in terms of customer benefits. While the goals may be aggressive, they are achievable with some effort. Unfortunately, many public libraries do not have a vision statement. It's as if "more of the same" is assumed to be just fine.

Strategies

Over the course of time, library services have evolved with little thought given as to what strategies might be employed to more effectively meet the needs of the library's customers. Initially libraries acquired, cataloged, and stored materials (this is often times referred to as the "warehousing approach" or the "just in case someone will like it strategy"). Access to collections migrated from closed stacks to open, which facilitates browsable searching by the library's customers. Further, as collections grew and library customer's encountered problems finding the desired materials, new library services such as references were introduced. Yet, rarely is there a fundamental discussion among librarians about what strategies would be most effective in a particular set of circumstances.

Asking "What if?" in a disciplined way allows you to consider the possibilities of tomorrow and then take action empowered by those provocations and insights. Clearly, public libraries are experiencing new and unforeseen challenges and opportunities. The question then becomes, "Is your library ready to act?"

Among the "What if?" questions that might be explored are: What alternatives exist to discontinue the use of traditional library shelving? What alternatives might we explore to revise or eliminate the Dewey Decimal system? What other options are there for organizing services (and what staff really should be delivering these services)? Should we eliminate reference desks? How might we involve our customers more intimately so that our library Web site is appealing and has a number of reasons to attract people to return again and again? Should we continue to call the library "the library"? How can we create a brand that better resonates with our community? Well, you get the idea. Consider topics and ideas that have never been examined before.

Some libraries have found that using scenarios is one effective method to explore some "out of the box" thinking as libraries consider their future. Peter Hernon and Joe Matthews explore the topic of the future of the library in a recent book called *Reflecting on the Future* (2013). Remember that strategic planning is all about answering the questions, "Where do we want to be?" and "How will we deliver services to our customers that are most responsive to their needs?"

Market Segments

As noted in chapter two, the library should identify the market segments it is going to serve and with what services as a part of its plan. Not all market segments will be served to the same degree or with the same range of services. For example, children's story hours will not appeal to the retired market segment. Explicitly identifying the services for each market segment and what market segments are more important than others is a fruitful process for any public library to complete.

Summary of Findings

In this chapter, we have learned when a library has reflected upon and developed a written statement of its mission, values, vision, and strategy for delivering services to its community, then all staff members will have a clear picture of what they are working to achieve. It makes decisions about how to develop a library's collection (physical and electronic) easier since the goals and objectives have been established and are articulated in written form.

Take Action

Your public library should:

- Prepare a document that identifies the strategies the library is currently following with regards to its physical collections, ways in which customers gain access to the physical collections, types of activities that can be performed within the building, the number and type of electronic resources available to customers from their home or office, the usefulness of the library's Web site.

- Develop an understanding of how the library's customers view the library. Consolidate the comments about the library from a number of different sources—social media, customer comment cards, customer satisfaction surveys, comments made to staff, and so forth as detailed by Peter Hernon and Joseph Matthews (2011).

- Consider how the library should address the various outside forces that are currently impacting the library. The library may wish to create a new strategy plan. The plan should carefully explore a variety of strategies to better meet the needs of various market segments.

4

The Physical Collection

The library is not a shrine for the worship of books. It is not a temple where literary incense must be burned or where one's devotion to the bound book is expressed in ritual. A library, to modify the famous metaphor of Socrates, should be the delivery room for the birth of ideas—a place where history comes to life.

—Norman Cousins

Traditionally, a library's collection has been the raison d'etre for the library. Indeed, the majority of people today view the public library as a warehouse for books. Any library's collection is driven by local perception of need and constrained by available resources. The purpose of a collection development policy is to balance available resources with the needs of the customers. Given the high costs associated with locating, requesting, moving, and delivering specific items from one location (or library) to another, libraries have traditionally sought to build large local collections (or as large as the building would allow). Any public library is able to judge how well it is doing by examining the use of its collections. The degree of customer satisfaction with a library's collection determines the amount of repeated use of the library. Developing, maintaining, and then discarding (weeding) a library's collection is an ongoing job that requires careful observation and wise decisions.

This chapter will answer the following set of questions:

- What are the available choices about the characteristics of the collection?

- What influences demand?

- What types of items should be in a collection?

- What costs does the customer incur when using the library?

45

What Are the Characteristics of the Collection?

Ask people in American what they think of when they think of a library (or public library) and they respond with a one-word answer—books! According to the OCLC report, "Perceptions" *of Libraries and Information Resources* (2005), the library brand is "books."

A "brand image" according to the American Marketing Association is "the perception of a brand in the minds of people. The brand image is a mirror reflection (though perhaps inaccurate) of the brand personality or product being considered. It is what people believe about a brand-—their thoughts, feelings, expectations." About 70 percent of the more than 3,700 respondents in the OCLC "Perceptions" study associate library first and foremost with books. There is no runner-up or close second. Interestingly, the report found that:

> The words *trust, authoritative*, and *privacy* were never mentioned. *Community* was mentioned in one response. *Quality* was mentioned twice. *Education* was mentioned four times; *learning* was mentioned nine times. *Free* was mentioned 70 times. *Books* were mentioned 2,152 times. (pages 3–33)

The overwhelming association of the library brand as books is not surprisingly reinforced by a great many public libraries who use some stylized version of the book as their library logo. The brand "books" is also bolstered by the American Library Association's multi-year campaign to foster reading (of books) by their use of celebrities appearing in the READ posters.

Librarians and frequent library customers know, of course, that the public library today offers a broad array of products and services. In order to build a broader brand image, the local public library must engage their current and potential customers using a variety of marketing techniques in order to "get the new library brand image out" to the community. It is also important to recognize that the image of a brand does not happen overnight with one marketing campaign but rather occurs over an extended period of time with the library presenting its new image and message at every possible opportunity.

What Influences User Selections?

For many individuals, the raison d'etre of a library is its collection. In their eyes, without a collection of books, CDs, DVD, and other materials, there is no library. The characteristics of a collection greatly influence the amount of use that it receives. If a library has relatively few materials that appeal to a community or if the materials are old and worn, then people will likely turn to other alternatives that are convenient and accessible.

Interestingly, an analysis of the twenty-three largest public libraries (excluding the New York Public Library and the Boston Public Library) found that 85 percent of their combined collections were only held by one to five libraries indicating that each library's collection contains unique materials (Lavoie 2011). However, it is likely that as the size of a public library's collection decreases in size, the amount of collection overlap will increase.

Fundamental questions that should be answered by every library include:

- What factors influence user selections?

- What mix of products (items in the collection) and services influence user selections?

- Does the life cycle of each product affect user selections?

Subject

Subject clearly matters for a majority of library customers. Customers come to the library knowing that they are interested in a book about a topic, or because they wish to select a DVD or . . . (you get the idea). Similarly, studies have found that a majority of people going to a bookstore to purchase nonfiction books based on a subject rather than having a particular title in mind (NPD Group 1996).

Several studies suggest that customers exhibit fairly consistent levels of interest in various topics, at least within similar geographic boundaries. Notably, a study of the usage of library materials at all of the branch facilities of the Indianapolis Marion County (IN) Public Library found similar circulation patterns of subjects in different branches (the branches are located in socioeconomically diverse neighborhoods) even though total circulation at each branch varied widely (Ottensmann et al. 1995). Similarly, Davis and Altman (1997) found comparable broad circulation patterns when examining circulation data from 11 public libraries serving varied socioeconomic populations.

Overlap studies are intended to identify the amount of duplication among a set of libraries while also identifying materials that are not duplicated. The amount of overlap varies by type of library and the number of libraries involved in the analysis. On average, the level of collection overlap for a group of public libraries ranges from 55 to 80 percent (Matthews 2007).

Yet, it cannot be denied that individual community characteristics have an impact on what is popular in any given library. It just stands to reason that books about boats and sailing are going to be more popular in coastal communities while books about mountains, hiking, skiing, and so forth are more popular in communities located adjacent to high hills and the mountains.

It is also true that special localized collections may have an increased appeal during times of periodic celebration (a centennial for example) than during other times. Such special collections may focus on a particular topic (e.g., horse racing, auto racing, surfing); a particular industry (e.g., automobiles, computers); a specific individual; the digitized images of historical newspapers and local magazines of interest to those interested in genealogy; as well as historical events (e.g., the Civil War, the civil rights struggle, and so forth). Some public libraries have such unique appeal that visitors often travel a great distance to view and use these rare resources—consider, for example, the New York Public Library, the Boston Public Library, the Seattle Public Library, and many more. The economic benefits from such collections and how such calculations are estimated were discussed in chapter three.

Age, sex, and other individual characteristics also influence subject interests. For example, older adults are more likely to read religious materials while enjoying a broader array of topics (Scales 1996, Delin et al. 1995). Willits and Willits (1991) found in a survey that rural public library customers were more interested in works on gardening, crafts, and religious works while their urban counterparts were more interested in classic works of fiction and nonfiction. Another survey found that members of larger communities were interested in science and business materials while the residents of smaller communities were interested in gardening, hobbies, and sports (Lucas 1982).

All of this suggests it is important to use summary information as a baseline but that each library should develop an exact profile of what interests its customers, using all available data.

Changing demographics in almost every community also affects public library services. In a survey by the Urban Libraries Council (2003) more than 75 percent of responding libraries claimed 30 or more countries of origin among their registered customers. Immigrant information needs, not surprisingly, are directed toward practical help for becoming settled in the United States. Recent immigrants desire information concerning citizenship, immigration law, location, and hours of immigration offices, necessary forms, and so forth. In addition, access to English as a Second Language (ESL) materials, language instruction software, conversation groups, and classes are also frequently requested. However, a survey by Burke (2008) found that immigrants were less likely to use non-English language materials, attend library programs, or to search for information compared to the findings of prior studies.

Usage data by subject areas (call number ranges) can be combined with holding data to compare the percent of circulation within a subject area with the percent of holdings in that area. If a significant gap between the two measures exists, it may be necessary for the library to either increase (or decrease) what it orders in this area. Also it would be helpful if libraries started using the subject heading information when preparing an analysis of usage of the collection. In addition to the obvious of what subject headings are used by user of the OPAC (and which are not) it could also be revealing if a library were to examine the amount of usage by each subject heading. And if a library allows the customers to add tags (not pre-coordinated words and phrases) to its OPAC, these additional words can then also be used for analysis.

As public libraries transition to become a digital library (or more of a digital library), it is important that they analyze all available usage statistics concerning the library's Web site as well as the electronic resources in order to provide a set of resources that have value to the library's customers.

Format

Clearly personal preference, along with lifestyle considerations, affects the choice of material format (book, audio book on CD, audio book on Playaway, large-print book, eBooks [and the many devices that allow someone to read the eBook], and so forth) that is borrowed by the library's customers. The continuing innovations that are entering the marketplace are placing increased pressures on library budget to spend more money on the same title (but provide the same title in multiple formats for the convenience of customers)—all at a time of reduced or stagnant library budgets.

While providing such variety was "cutting edge" several years ago, the vast majority of public libraries now routinely provide customers with several choices when it comes to material formats:

- Digital audio book on iPods or MP3 players (Playaway)
- Audio book on CDs
- Large print books
- eBooks
- DVDs
- Video games
- Graphic novels
- Video-on-demand (downloading)
- And so forth

Many libraries have found that responding to customer demand for new material formats is attracting non-users to the library for the first time. And, as these individuals become more comfortable in the library setting, they will branch out and try borrowing materials in other formats as well as use other library services and programs.

The Audio Publishers Association reported that the number of available audio book now exceeds six thousand, that audio book downloads account for about 52 percent of unit sales, and that while the CD format is still very popular unit sales are declining.[1] The audiences for audio books include commuters, vacationers, truckers, sales people, and others who spend considerable time on the road. Fiction, in all of its various guises, is more popular than nonfiction titles in audio format.

While it is clear that DVDs and Blu-ray players will eventually vanish as people transition to streaming services for content, borrowing DVDs from libraries is still a popular activity. In many libraries the circulation of DVDs continues to increases on a year-to-year basis. But the trend is clearly moving from borrowing a physical disc (atoms) to downloading of content (bits)—consider the growing popularity of Netflix.

In a recent survey, 27 percent of respondents indicated that borrowing movies from the library was their primary source of such contentdown from 36 percent the previous year (Enis 2012). DVD borrowing can account for up to 40 to 50 percent of circulation in many libraries (and holdings range from 10 to 20 percent). Clearly the trend of moving to streaming is already having a significant impact on the library and its circulation figures. Notably, several studies have suggested that the environmental costs from moving from atoms (and the costs of traveling to the library to borrow a DVD) to streaming media are less overall (Anderson 2010).

A recent *Library Journal* survey found that public libraries spend about 59 percent of their material acquisitions budget on books and 12 percent on DVDs as shown in Figure 4.1 (Hoffert 2013). Given the appeal that specific material formats have for a unique market segment, it is possible to design effective yet inexpensive marketing campaigns that appeal to and attract both existing and new customers to the library.

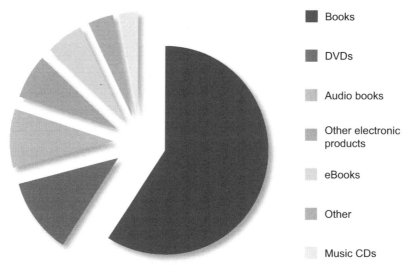

Figure 4.1. Materials Budget Breakdown

Currency (Newness)

It is no real surprise to any librarian who works in a public library that new materials circulate at much higher rates than older materials. Customers want current materials, especially in areas of constant innovation and change such as computers, hardware, and software applications that use the Internet, current events, politics, the best seller lists, and so forth. And in many cases, having older materials that contain obsolete or wrong information is a disservice to the library's users.

However, retaining (or even adding) older materials to the collection can be advantageous. For example, fiction readers who have discovered a "new" author may be interested in reading all of the author's works. Libraries used to have concerns about retaining older materials, especially the classics, but today there are so many options for someone interested in the classics (Amazon, Half. com, online used book stores, and so forth) that the library can relinquish this responsibility. After all, shelf space is simply too precious to retain works that rarely, if ever, circulate. Remember that classics and older titles are available in eBook format from free Web sites such as Project Gutenberg.

A recent survey among book readers at Goodreads indicated that the books they are most likely to read next are influenced by a trusted friend (25 percent), everyone talking about it (20 percent), a book club (15 percent), reviews on Goodreads (12 percent), and "best lists" (9 percent).

In addition, displays of new materials experience significantly higher circulation rates than if new materials are immediately shelved with the rest of the collection.

And even more important is getting the new materials ordered, received, processed, and into the hands of the library customer. Linda Speas (2012) reported the results of a project to analyze the reasons why new materials were taking a fairly long period of time before they appeared on the shelves of the Arapahoe (C) Library District and then the actions taken to significantly reduce this time period.

Genre

The genre of a work can have a significant impact on the choice of the customer as whether an item will be used or ignored. Genre is a category of artistic composition, be it music or literature, characterized by similarities in form, style, or subject matter. A study by Yu and O'Brien (1999) found that genre and the author's name were the two main methods by which library patrons discover fiction. Popularity of genres varies by gender as well as age and language. For example, the younger you are the more likely science fiction, fantasy, and horror will appeal; while if you are older, history, war, genealogy, and biography/ autobiography genres will be interesting.

Table 4.1. Most Popular Book Genres by Gender

Women			Men	
Place	Genre	% Favorite Genre	Genre	% Favorite Genre
1	Mystery, suspense, detective, spy, adventure	24%	Science fiction, fantasy, horror	17%
2	Romance	12%	Mystery, suspense, detective, spy, adventure	14%
3	Science fiction, fantasy, horror	8%	History, war, genealogy, heritage	9%
4	Personal growth	8%	Science and technology	7%

From *Reading and Buying Books for Pleasure: 2005 National Survey Final Report*. Courtesy of the Department of Canadian Heritage. Reproduced with the permission of the Minister of Public Works and Government Services Canada, 2013.

When fiction books are labeled and shelved in separate genre groupings, circulation increases. This is true for print books as well as for audio books, videos, and other formats. Tracking usage of a library's collection by genre is important, but it is also important to ensure that each genre collection has recently published materials so that it will appeal to the customer.

One national survey (Heritage Canada 2005) found that the most popular genre is that of the action novel (detective, spy, mystery, suspense, and adventure) as shown in Table 4.1. Others would suggest that romance is the most popular genre based on actual sales. Obviously the popularity of a particular genre in each community will vary somewhat from the national averages. Herald (2013) has suggested the use of seven genre groups or categories:

- Science fiction
- Fantasy
- Horror
- Crime/Mystery
- Historical Fiction
- Westerns
- Thrillers/Adventure
- Romance

- Women's Lives

- Nonfiction

- Mainstream

In addition, Herald has suggested three emerging reading interests: inspirational/Christian, urban fiction, and graphic novels.

After visiting just a few public libraries it becomes clear that each library develops their genre categories (the author has noted as many as sixteen genre categories in one library and as few as four in others). Diana Herald maintains a Web site with a discussion and links to other genre resources.[2] There are a host of other books, Web sites, and electronic discussion groups that provide additional information about a broad cross section of genres that focus on a single genre (see for example Saricks 2001).

Analyzing the use of a library's collection by genre should be conducted on an annual basis. This will assist librarians in understanding how changes in fiction trends and reading desires are affecting the use of their collections in a specific area.

Awareness of Author/Title

How well an author is known, especially when it comes to contemporary authors, affects book sales as well as circulation of their works at the local public library. It is not uncommon for an author's latest work to attract considerable interest even before the work is published. Some libraries allow customers to place holds for new and/or popular works and for some authors this may mean that the hold queue is several hundred names long.

Yu and O'Brien (1999) group adult fiction readers into three interesting groups:

1. *Author-bound readers* track all works by a limited number of authors (often within the same genre) and do not accept replacement authors

2. *Author-oriented readers* may prefer a subset of authors but will accept the works of other writers when their first choice is unavailable

3. *Author-free readers* are agnostic when it comes to specific authors and are willing to try unfamiliar authors and titles.

Library customers may be more familiar with a work's title than the author or actor's name. For example, some 85 percent of a public library's customers selecting videos were interested in a particular title or work. In other situations, the customer may be interested in new works for a specific series within a genre—medieval romance, traditional regency romance, victorian romance, American historical romance, rontier western, and so forth.

Obviously the amount and type of publicity given to a work influences the likelihood that a library customer has heard about it and will want to borrow the item. Works featured in newspapers, magazines, Internet reviews, television, radio talk shows, book signings, and so forth will have more name recognition and thus result in demand for the work by library customers. Among the many sources of such information are:

- The *Library Journal* Pre-Pub Alert
- *Publishers Weekly* Forecasts and Rights columns, publisher advertisements
- *Publishers Weekly* and *Kirkus Reviews* provide information about author tours and large promotional budgets
- *Get Ready Sheet,* a bimonthly newsletter that provides information on promotional budgets, author interviews, and movie tie-ins
- The American Booksellers Association Web site—check the Media Guide in particular.

Of particular note, the Oprah Winfrey Book Club has featured many titles over the years and her persuasive influence, for books and other products, has come to be known as the "Oprah Effect" (Maryles 2000). Some libraries have created Oprah Book Club spine stickers, created an "Oprah" shelf, and even added "Oprah book" as a subject heading in the cataloging record.

Style and Appeal

Within publishing, style usually refers to a distinctive tone, rhythms, or mode of expression that characterize the work of a particular writer so that a particular style stands out from others in a specific genre or subject area. Just consider the different styles found when reading a typical article published in *American Libraries* or *College & Research Libraries* or *Library Journal* or *USA Today*.

Clearly style is influenced by how detailed or intricate a plot is, how well developed the characters are, the use of dialect, use of imagery, dialogue, pacing, sense of humor, as well as a number of other characteristics of a work. Prior research suggests that library patrons are interested in books with a "good plot," interesting and absorbing characters, a style that moves the reader along at an appropriate pace, and use book jacket reviews to help decide if an item should be borrowed or not (Spiller 1980, Ross and Chelton 2001).

Joyce Saricks (2005) asserts that readers have style preferences that relate to story (plot), character, frame (setting), and language and she calls this "appeals theory." Nancy Pearl and Sarah Cords (2010) found this approach particularly useful with "mainstream" fiction (often referred to as "general" fiction vs. genre fiction).

Different styles appeal to different people; what some may consider important will barely register with another user. Regardless, library patrons consider style as important criteria when selecting materials to borrow. One popular tool that can assist the library patron (and librarian) select other works in a similar style is *NoveList*. Others include Bowker's *Fiction/Nonfiction Connection*, and Gale's *Books and Authors*.

Critical Acclaim or Excellence

Within the library arena, critical acclaim is usually considered to be the degree of aesthetic or artistic excellence it possesses. Librarians purchase titles that are thoughtful or insightful, cover significant topics, are clearly written, present factual information accurately (while acknowledging sources), and possess literary merit.

Librarians often create displays of materials that have won awards, include award information within the catalog record, or place stickers "Award Winners" on the spine or front cover of an item. The extent to which customers are interested in an item's critical acclaim is unknown. At the root of the selection process for a public library is the ongoing debate revolving around the issue of "quality versus demand." Charles Robinson, the former director of the Baltimore County Public Library, initiated this debate in the 1980s when he announced that the selection policy for the library would be to "give 'em what they want." This resulted in the multibranch library system ordering hundreds of copies of best sellers to meet customer demand.

Studies that have attempted to determine the relative use of "critical acclaim" items compared to the rest of the collection have resulted in mixed messages. In general, critical acclaim items seem to circulate roughly in the same proportion as their percent of total holdings. However, it is clear that large advertising campaigns do positively affect book sales and reader demand (Rosen 2003). And near-field communication technology can offer the customer with an online mobile device discount coupons, reviews, and other pertinent information that influences the demand for books (Webb 2012).

Not surprisingly, people's reading preferences fluctuate over time as their needs and moods vary. Ross and Chelton (2001) found that during hectic times, library patrons tend to rely on familiar authors and subjects while during times of more calm that they will be more adventurous in their selection of materials. And user-provided reviews of books at Amazon.com and Barnesandnoble.com do influence sales, especially reviews that are noted as helpful by other users (Chevalier and Mayzlin 2003).

All of this suggests that having a grounded understanding of the various customer segments that use the library will assist the library in making better selections as materials are being added to the collection (and also as items are being withdrawn from the collection).

Language

Research has shown, not surprisingly, that people prefer to read in their primary language. Larger urban libraries, with much higher populations of immigrants from various countries, typically have large collections on non-English language materials. In these larger libraries, the online catalog (as well as the library's Web site) is accessible using several non-English languages.

Foreign language materials typically are grouped together and these materials have higher circulation rates if they are easily accessible and displayed using merchandizing face-out displays (Envirosell 2007a, 2007b, 2008).

Individuals who prefer materials in a foreign language clearly represent a unique and distinctive market segment. The Richmond (British Columbia) Public Library has an extensive Chinese immigrant population (representing about 40 percent of the city's population). Understandably, the library has a large Chinese language collection that is well used. In addition, the library has installed a materials dispensing machine within the library where customers can borrow and return Chinese-language DVDs.

Packaging

Publishers (as well as product manufacturers) have long recognized that exciting packaging makes a significant difference in sales. Book covers and the front of other products are all carefully designed to attract attention and increase their visibility. The crowded field of series paperbacks has been successful, in part, because of their appealing and unique book jackets. Children's and youth librarians have long recognized that that cover designs greatly influence the selection choices made by young people.

Cover art and the use of teasers (brief reviews) have influenced those who purchase books as well as choose to borrow materials from the library. Those selecting videos are often influenced by the plot information provided on the back of the DVD, the list of actors involved, or the name of the director/producer.

Obviously it is in the library's interest to retain as much of the item's original packaging (given the investment made by the publisher) so that the library's customers have access to the information they need to make selection decisions.

Listening (Programming)

A majority of public libraries offer programs designed to entertain, educate, and encourage discussion. The interesting challenge for any library is to determine the degree to which a program can be linked to the resources available within the library's collection. Some libraries track the use of a collection related to a program's topic as one indicator of the value and usefulness of the program to the attendees. Whether the program is created and offered by library staff, hired storytellers, volunteers, an author reading, an expert, and so forth, evaluating the program's utility must include more than simply a count as to the number of people who attend.

Given today's economy, programs related to job skills, job finding, preparation of a resume, completing an online job application, and so forth are all fairly popular in terms of attendance and responding to a community's needs.

The range of programs that can be offered by a library is only limited by ones imagination (and the budget of course). In addition to children's story times, programs offered by various public libraries have included theme-oriented sessions (westerns, mysteries, puzzles, pets, animals, and so forth); book discussion clubs; science fiction, horror, and fantasy stories; plays; travel; home improvement; food tasting and cooking; musical performances; puppet shows and so forth.

Some libraries use their Web sites to promote and offer online book clubs, summer reading programs, blogs, and so forth. The idea is to reach out to different market segments so that the customer can participate wherever they are (traveling to the library physically is not required).

More than 90 percent of public libraries offer classes on general Internet use and general computer skills (note that these classes might be taught by staff or knowledgeable volunteers). Many of these classes distribute lists of recommended readings so the participants can improve their skills. As such, public libraries play an important role in bridging the digital divide.[3]

What's Best for the Customer?

In order to maximize customer satisfaction, the professional staff must make informed decisions about what is the right mix of products—meeting space, Internet computers, books, DVDs, audio materials, children's books, and so forth as well as the amount of materials in each category to include in the library's collection. The real challenge, of course, is that over the course of time the mix will change as products go through their life cycle, and community tastes and needs change in response to the greater technological and societal changes that take place.

And the need to review the mix must take into account the number (and size) of each library branch location. Librarians need to periodically review a series of reports in order to evaluate their current mix of products in order to determine what changes should be made. These reports (available from the library's integrated library system) should identify:

- Types of materials (and items) heavily used by customers

- Types of materials (and items) infrequently or never used by customers

- Comparison of percent of material type to percent of circulation by material type

- Review of requests made by patrons for items to be purchased by the library

Clearly, a responsive customer-focused library is going to attempt to provide the materials that are in high demand to their customers. This may mean additional copies of titles in high demand as well as adding more materials in a particular subject area. While a library can often be responsive in terms of adding additional materials to a collection, in some cases, existing space (or other) limitations may prevent adding computer workstations or group study space to a specific library.

Weeding a library's collection is one of those professional responsibilities that, despite the best of intentions, is rarely completed in a timely manner. A fair amount of research has demonstrated that a well-weeded collection experiences higher circulation levels than keeping the shelves "chock full." In addition to weeding rarely or infrequently used materials, it is sometimes necessary to completely remove a type of material that no longer has value—videotapes, microfilm collections, and so forth.

Examination of the non-circulating items (as well as the low-circulating items) can offer information about use of these information resources. For example, Pierce (2003) found that some subject areas of apparent non-use might reflect a sort of use through users' failure to return (or even checkout) these materials. Pierce found that young adults intentionally remove items in the seven hundreds as well as reading nonfiction for pleasure. Young adults are also likely to heavily use comics and music (Vaillancourt 2002).

The theft and non-return of materials can be a significant problem as was noted recently when the Austin (TX) Public Library reported that they had lost more than one million dollars of materials over a five-year period (Plohetski and Pierrotti 2013). Charles Martell (2010) has suggested that libraries should be more proactive in dealing with titles that are likely never to be returned after checkout by:

- Seeing if the title is available online
- If a high-risk title is available online, stop purchasing paper copies
- Restrict high-risk print titles to "Library Use Only"
- Increase the speed with which overdue notices are sent out, empathize the penalties if the item is not returned, and send the customer to a collection agency much faster. For every day an overdue, non-returned item is not returned, the likelihood it will ever be returned moves quickly to zero.

One of the realities facing public libraries today is that it is no longer necessary to assume responsibility for maintaining copies of library materials (with the exception of rare items that have long-term cultural or historical significance). Anyone can now purchase, often at a very low cost, items that have a very specialized focus using such Internet resources as Amazon, eBay, online used bookstores, and so forth. In addition, the digitization of more than fifteen million books by Google (as well as the other digitization projects that provide online access to even more materials) means that a great deal of material is now immediately accessible at the fingertips of an individual.

What Costs Does the Customer Incur?

Given all of the potential factors that a customer may use in making a selection about what materials to use or borrow from the library, the customer is still faced with the need to solve a puzzle. The puzzle is that the customer must learn how various materials and resources are located within the library. The ability of the customer to navigate within the library using both signage and other clues provided by the library (color of walls, carpets, general layout, and so forth) is critical to their success in using the library.

Everyone makes a conscious decision about how they will spend their time and consider the value of alternative activities before making a choice. People consider the costs (actual out-of-pocket as well as their time) and the likely benefits they will receive. People recognize that there are alternatives to using the physical or virtual library. As they decide whether the library is providing or not providing sufficient value, they thus decide to use or not use the library.

Prices

Some libraries have set prices (fees) for specific (often high-demand) services such as borrowing DVDs and placing holds for popular materials. Other libraries have decided to position themselves at the other extreme of the fines/

fees continuum by doing away with all fines and fees. Should a library decide to charge a fine or fee there are two approaches that can be followed:

- *Cost-recovery pricing* attempts to determine the actual costs associated with providing a service and the likely demand and then calculating a cost per use in order to recover the library's costs. For example, assume a DVD costs the library twenty dollars and it incurs additional costs of ten dollars per copy to catalog and process. In addition, the library estimates that a DVD has a useful life of sixty viewing. Thus, dividing the total cost of thirty dollars per DVD by the anticipated use of sixty results in a fee of fifty cents per DVD checkout to the library customer. In this way, the library recovers their costs of providing this service and those that actually use the service are directly paying for the service.

- *Demand-oriented pricing* can be used as an alternative. Library staff estimates the value to the user for a particular service (taking into consideration the available competitive options and their associated prices) and sets the price (fee) accordingly. In this case, a DVD rental fee of one dollar would seem to be competitive and would result in additional revenue for the library (assuming the same amount of use as the price set using the cost recovery method).

Another form of demand-oriented pricing is the recognition that the demand for some types of materials is greater than others and thus the library sets different overdue fines that varies by type of material. For example, some libraries will charge twenty-five cents per day for each overdue DVD while only charging ten cents per day for an overdue book.

Another form of demand-driven pricing is the time period that different types of materials may be borrowed from the library. For example, high demand materials (DVDs), new and popular fiction, and titles on the "best seller" lists, may have shorter checkout periods than older items in the collection that experience less demand.

It should be noted that the fines and fees collected by many public libraries actually comprise a significant component of the library's annual operating budget and the reduction or elimination of some or all of these revenues would have a major impact of the quality of library services.

Out-of-Pocket Costs

Library customers incur a wide variety of costs that often are not considered or are ignored by a library. This section identifies and discusses some of the more important aspects of both out-of-pocket and convenience costs. Among the out-of-pocket costs to select and return materials or participate in an event are:

- *Getting there*. The actual costs of gasoline and other components of operating an automobile needed to drive to the library. Other costs for some patrons might include bus fare, money for a parking meter, reimbursement for low-income residents who wish to visit the library, and so forth.

- *Fines and fees*. A fine is used as a stick or incentive to encourage customers to return borrowed materials in a timely manner. Some libraries allow a grace period before the daily fine for overdue materials begin to accumulate. A library uses fees to moderate demand for popular (and often expensive) services. For many customers, perhaps a majority, fees are generally supported (especially during periods of fiscal constraint).

- *Non-resident fee*. Many libraries charge a non-resident fee for those who live outside the official service deliver area (city boundary). Most libraries will charge a fee that is roughly equivalent to the actual per capita support for the library's budget. In addition to determining the per capita support, some libraries calculate the per household support for the library in order to determine the non-resident fee. In addition, some libraries provide a "temporary" library card valid for a short period of time so that the individual need not pay the non-resident fee.

  Some libraries have developed reciprocal borrowing agreements between other nearby libraries so a library card is "valid" in other nearby libraries avoiding the need for a non-resident fee. In addition, some states have provided financial support, typically using federal funds, in the form of a partial reimbursement for the direct borrowing of materials from individuals who live outside the local library boundary.

- *Rental fees*. Public libraries have long used rental fees for a variety of services. Among the more popular library rental fee-based services are: duplicate copies of best-selling book titles; audio books; DVDs; borrowing of art prints, household tools, materials-by-mail service, custom research, meeting rooms, auditoriums, and so forth.

- *Holds and interlibrary loan fees*. Some libraries charge to place a hold (reserve) for popular materials in an attempt to moderate the demand for such materials. Other libraries typically charge an interlibrary loan fee, as the borrowing of materials from other libraries (near and far) is an expensive proposition for both the borrowing and lending library.

- *Fees for lost or damaged items.* Almost all libraries have a policy in place whereby the customer is financially responsible (to some degree) for lost or damaged items. Many libraries change the total (original or replacement) cost of lost items and may also include an additional charge for the processing of the replacement item. Some libraries allow staff to reduce or waive fines when faced with extenuating circumstances in order to maintain the customer's good will ("The dog ate it!").

Convenience Costs

In addition to actual out-of-pocket costs, the library customer will also experience other costs that are called convenience costs. As Adam Smith famously observed, "The real price of everything, what everything really costs to the man who wants to acquire it, is the toil and trouble of acquiring it" (1937). Clearly the library and the customer influence the amount of time an individual spends in the library. For the library, decisions about the number of branch locations, the hours of service, types of service, the convenience in using the library (wayfinding), and so forth significantly influence the amount of time spent in the library.

Among the more important convenience costs are:

- *Obtaining a Library Card.* The time and effort needed to obtain a library card can often be frustrating from the customer's perspective. Is the library card application paper-based or available online? Is the application available in multiple languages? Is there a line to obtain a library card? What personal identification information must be shared with the library in order to verify the customer's identity?

- *Locating Desired Items in the Collection.* Attempting to locate a specific item within the library can be very aggravating for the individual, especially if they are not that familiar with the library's layout and location of specific collections. In short, from the customer's perspective, the library has erected a number of hurdles that must be overcome before the customer is successful.

  Making the assumption that the customer will use the online catalog is fraught with difficulties. A relatively small proportion of the people entering the library use the online catalog (Envirosell 2007a, 2008). And of those attempting to use the catalog, only a slight majority of people will be successful (keyword searching has improved the searching experience). Thus some percent of people will be unsuccessful and frustrated in their effort to locate a desired item. The library's solution to this frustrating experience is to provide training classes or to station staff nearby so that they can provide assistance when needed. Online catalog research has demonstrated that people will walk out of the library without the desired item rather than approaching staff (and appearing to be stupid).

Many come to the library and have no idea of a specific author or title but rather have a general notion of what they want (Something about home repairs, building a deck, getting a good mystery book, a new DVD, and so forth). Thus, these people really want to browse the collection to find items of interest and yet the library has the collection "hidden" in call number order on traditional library shelving in spine out order. The fact that many people don't get the "Dewey thing" has meant that some libraries have moved to merchandising the collection with items placed face out—the Markham (Ontario, Canada) Public Library, the Richmond (British Columbia, Canada) Public Library, the Anythink Libraries (CO), among others.

- *But I Can't Find It!* In some libraries, collections are not logically organized and high interest items are not located close to the front entrance. Thus, how the library "explains" where various collections and services are located becomes key. The explanation takes place using signage (often large colorful signs to identify a broad topic or collection) as well as colors and textures (floors and walls). This explanation from the customer's perspective is usually referred to as "wayfinding."

  Once the customer has found the appropriate area or shelving, the item may or may not be on the shelf. The many reasons customers may not find the item (checked out, waiting to be reshelved, mis-shelved, stolen, and so forth) are explored in greater detail in *The Measurement and Evaluation of Library Services*—see chapter eight (Matthews 2007). Based on a number of research studies, the "availability" of an item ranges from 50 to 75 percent in most public libraries. That means that the customer has a one in two to a three out of four chance of finding the item! Not really great odds.

- *Borrowing Materials.* Should a customer need to stand in line in order to borrow materials, especially if they have to wait "too long," then the experience of visiting the library is dismal. In the retail environment, Paco Underhill (1999) found that the waiting time was the single most important aspect in determining the customer's perception of the quality of service they received. Obviously what is "too long" varies from person to person.

Many libraries have moved to implement self-checkout machines, which can substantially alleviate the checkout lines. Some libraries have achieved their goal of having 90 percent or more of materials being checked out, done directly by the customer using the self-checkout machines (McNeely 2000).

• *Returning Borrowed Items.* Almost every library (that has branch locations) will absorb some of the costs of returning borrowed items by allowing the customer to return the items to any location (the library assumes the responsibility for moving the returned items to the "correct" or "home" location. Placing material return drops outside the library allows the customer to return the items without having to leave their automobile.

Customers also experience a convenience cost when they must return an item before they have finished with that item. Almost all libraries allow a customer to renew an item (provided no other customers are waiting in a queue to use the item). Many libraries allow customers to renew items by phone or via the Internet. Items with shorter loan periods, e.g., two weeks, experience renewal rates that are considerably higher than items with longer loan rates (Goldhor 1990).

• *Filling Reserve Requests.* Many public libraries allow customers to place a hold or reserve for popular items in a collection. The result is a holds queue (first come, first served). The fact that customers must wait for popular items is a real aggravation for many. From the library's perspective, this process is automated using the integrated library system, thus sparing staff time to complete the process.

The delay in receiving the requested item can often be lengthy, depending upon the popularity of an item and the number of copies that the library has purchased. Many libraries have purchase alerts so that when the ratio of the number of holds to the number of copies already owned, the library is informed and staff can decide if they will purchase additional copies to reduce the overall wait time.

And the final convenience costs are those associated with traveling to pick up the desired items once the library has informed the customer that it is their turn (notices might be made by phone, an email, or mail notice).

Many customers are simply unwilling to accrue the convenience costs of waiting for an item and will settle for something else in the library or purchase the desired item from an online or physical retailer (given the popularity of Amazon clearly more and more people are deciding to purchase materials online).

- *Ordering Items From Another Location.* Many libraries allow their customer to place a "hold" for an item owned by the library that is on the shelf at another location. The desired item is then pulled from the shelf by library staff, and moving the item to the desired pickup location. For some libraries, this delivery service happens within 24 hours. The transportation costs for this service can be quite high, especially if the number of branch locations is high. In addition, to the out-of-pocket costs, the customer is inconvenienced due to the fact that the item is no longer on the shelf and thus cannot be "selected" by another customer. The expensive delivery costs is encouraging some libraries to consider the use of "floating collections"—discussed elsewhere (chapter seven) in greater detail in this book.

- *Interlibrary Loan Requests.* Relatively few customers utilize a service whereby the library requests a desired item from another library. This interlibrary loan service entails several delays, from the customer's perspective, as they need to request the item, have the library request the items from another library, wait for the item to arrive, be informed of the item's availability for pickup, and actually visit the library to pick up the item. In some cases, the overall wait time can range from two to four weeks (or longer) before the desired item is in the hands of the customer. In addition, the interlibrary loan service for books is expensive (in terms of staff time and shipping costs) for both the requesting and lending library. The costs and time delays have been reduced significantly for copies of journal articles as typically the article is scanned and transmitted electronically (either to the library or directly to the customer). Many libraries attempt to discourage or moderate use of this service by charging a fee.

Summary of Findings

Libraries work hard to minimize the impact of their policies and procedures on their customers but the end result is that the customer experiences real out-of-pocket and convenience costs when attempting to use the library. The goal should be to "walk in the shoes" of the customer and periodically review the actual impact of library policies and see if improvements can be made to make things easier for the customer in order to reduce the convenience costs for the customer.

Take Action

There are a number of actions your library should consider in order to improve the quality of services pertaining to the library's physical collections. Among these are:

- Run a report to compare percent of use to percent of holdings, by material type. Make adjustments to the acquisition's budget as needed.

- Run a report to compare percent of use to percent of holdings, by genre. Make adjustments to the acquisitions budget as needed.

- Provide a way for library customers to recommend books and other materials for the library to purchase. The suggestion form should be available in paper and online.

- Run a report indicating low usage for each item (less than two uses in the last year) and remove the items from the collection.

- Consider moving most, if not all of a library's collection, to merchandising shelving rather than continuing to use traditional library shelving.

- Consider providing a patron initiated interlibrary loan rather than the paper-based system now in place.

- Consider moving from the Dewey system to a bookstore-based approach to organizing the library collections.

Notes

1. The Audio Publishers Association conducts a Sales Survey on an annual basis. More information available at http://www.audiopub .org/

2. The Genreflecting Web site may be found at http://www.genrefluent .com/links.htm

3. Information about the Internet and public libraries is available at the University of Maryland's Information Policy & Access Center (http://ipac.umd.edu/publications?project=32).

The Virtual Library

Doing research on the Web is like using a library assembled piecemeal by pack rats and vandalized nightly.

—Roger Ebert

Are you placing enough interesting, freakish, long shot, weirdo bets?

—Tom Peters

Every public library is facing unrelenting pressure to provide access to an increasing number of electronic books, journals, and digital collections. For the customer, having desktop access as well as anytime, anywhere access to information using handheld devices has become a normal expectation. Thus, some proportion of the library's customers is invisible to the library—they use the library's Web site, the library's online catalog, and electronic resources (electronic journals, eBooks, and so forth) without ever visiting the library. To demonstrate that these customers are happy and return to the online library time after time, the usability of these online systems must be high.

Yet, the library's Web site and the set of online tools available to the customer are not the first destination among the vast majority of the residents in a community. Other Internet-based competitors provide systems that are easier to use and provide access to information that is convenient and whose quality is "good enough." Evidence for this state of affairs can be found from many sources. The OCLC *Perceptions* study (2005, 2010) found that 84 percent of people use search engines to begin information searches (library Web sites are the first destination of choice for only 1 percent of the respondents). The principle reason for this is the ease of use when using a search engine (Google for most people).

One of the consistent findings from a number of studies as well as anecdotal evidence is that convenience trumps everything! It is possible to view convenience as the behaviors people exhibit when they are engaged in the information-seeking process. A framework for better understanding the related theoretical approaches understanding convenience includes rational choice theory (Green 2002), short periods of attention (Connaway et al. 2011), and satisficing behavior (Prabha et al. 2007). In short, good enough information is almost always "good enough." As Peter Morville (2005) has noted:

> Numerous studies have shown users are often willing to sacrifice information quality for accessibility. This fast food approach to information consumption drives librarians crazy. "Our information is healthier and tastes better too" they shout. But nobody listens. We're too busy Googling.

Among the topics to be covered in this chapter are:

- The library's Web site
- The library's online catalog
- Electronic resources
- Apps

The Library Web Site

The whole experience of using a Web site is tied to a variety of factors, including how the site is organized and what navigation features—such as buttons, tabs, menus, links, graphics, site maps, and a site search engine—are provided. When they are visiting a Web site, users have a set of expectations; in order to be successful, the Web site must either meet or exceed those expectations. High-quality Web sites provide information and content of value to the customer that is easy to use!

A library's Web site offers access to the online catalog as well as other electronic resources accessible through the library. It provides information about the library, including locations, hours, upcoming events, and so forth. Every library should be able to answer a very fundamental question: What is the library's Web site for? Who are you trying to serve? What are your customers attempting to do when they visit your library's Web site? The reality is that every library has noble aspirations for their Web site by attempting to provide access to information (often a great deal of information) but does so in ways that haven't changed much since the introduction of the Internet.

A library's Web site may be in transition from one to another of three stages:

- **We are here.** The Web site provides basic library information, such as locations and hours, and allows the user to perform a few rudimentary tasks.

- **User-centered Web site.** In addition to gaining access to the library's online catalog and other electronic resources, the user is able to accomplish a variety of other tasks—place a hold, change a mailing address, submit a request for purchase, place an interlibrary loan request, interact directly with a reference librarian, and so forth.

- **Personalization.** The user is able to customize the "look and feel" of the Web site. For example, the user has a standing request to be placed in the hold queue as new books by a particular author, genre, and so forth are added to the collection.

A survey of library and museum Web sites found that the organizations believed that the focus was shifting from the size or uniqueness of their collections to services. Most of the organizations had not developed written goals and objectives for their Web sites, and the use of Web analytic tools revealed that the online user was very different than the people who physically visited the library (CLIR 2000). An analysis of library Web sites found that very little space is devoted to information resources, services, and information tools while marketing and design elements take up the largest proportion of the Web page (Kasperek et al. 2011). In addition, many library Web sites contain resources that are not discoverable by search engine Web crawlers (software that reports what content is accessible via a Web site). Thus, hiding the library jewels under a bushel basket is not a recommended practice.

One analysis of a library Web site found that users had problems because too much expert knowledge was expected of them, and use of library terminology contributed to their difficulties (Dickstein and Mills 2000). Table 5.1 presents a comparison of terminology that didn't work with the wording preferred by users. John Kupersmith[1] summarized forty-seven usability studies and found that:

- The average user success rate for finding journal articles is only 53 percent;

- The terms most often misunderstood by users include "acronyms and brand names, database, E-journals, index, periodical or serial, resource, reference and interlibrary loan;" and

- Terms most often understood by users include "find books; find articles" and terms accompanied by additional words or mouse overs that expand on their meaning.

Table 5.1. Evaluation of Library Terminology

What didn't work: Terms misunderstood, not understood, or not preferred	What did work: Terms understood or preferred
Databases—without referring to magazines, periodicals, or articles	The word *articles* prominently displayed as part of an icon representing periodicals and newspapers
Pathfinders	*Research by subject*
Web guides	*Tutorials*
Databases—described by one individual as "the base that holds the data"	*Finding an article*
Browse vs. Keyword	*Titles begins with . . .* *Subject begins with . . .*
Resources—No one used the word resources to describe anything	
Database finder . . .	*Find articles*
Circulation	*Borrowing*
Online databases and indexes	*Find articles*
Title words *Title browse*	*Title keywords* *Title begins with*
Database—Is it a spreadsheet?	*Find articles*

In short, a quick glance at most public library Web sites reveals that:

- The library is a roadblock that gets in the way of the user's attempt to accomplish a specific task
- The roadblock is characterized by Web sites with too many words
- Too much jargon
- Too many hidden links
- Links that do not work

Part of the challenge is to recognize that most Web sites are designed by librarians, who are quite knowledgeable and can deal with complexity, when in reality the actual user is someone who is not comfortable attempting to use a complicated Web site. The result is that the user becomes frustrated and angry and moves to other more user-friendly Web sites to gain access to information. Matthew Reidsma (2012) came up with a wonderful title for his presentation— "Your Library Website Stinks & It's Your Fault." He suggests the following activities in order to remake the library's Web site so that it meets the needs of the customer:

- Really listen to your customers (might use a focus group or two to accomplish this)

- As the library makes changes (it's not an all-or-nothing project) ask the customer for feedback

- Conduct usability tests—at least monthly

- Write concisely and clearly

- Use Web analytics, such as Google Analytics, to determine what pages are being used and which ones are ignored

- Test, revise, test again, revise again, etc.

Perhaps the most important aspect of a library's Web site is the response time experienced by users when they are downloading a Web page. The average amount of time a person is willing to wait for a Web page to load has decreased to just two seconds (Nah 2004).

About two-thirds of the wait time for the typical Web page download is local—time spent on the browser and operating system of the desktop computer or handheld device. Thus, if a Web page uses a fair number of graphic images or uses software outside of HTML, then the user is going to wait longer. The implication for your library's Web site is clear: make sure you optimize your Web site for speed!

Some public libraries have been working to improve the usability of their Web sites so that they provide more value to their users. Sample library Web sites that have improved usability are shown in Figure 5.1. Aaron Schmidt (2013) has recommended that a library's Web site should be designed in a way that helps people accomplish their tasks, and bibliographic data exists in the background and is shared only when it is useful. Remember that the goal of improving the usability of any Web site is to increase the users' quality of life by eliminating a lot of frustration and the feeling of inadequacy that follows every time someone is stumped when using the Web site.

Today's OPAC and Beyond

The library's online catalog, sometimes called an OPAC (Online Public Access Catalog), is not going to go away any time soon, despite the many

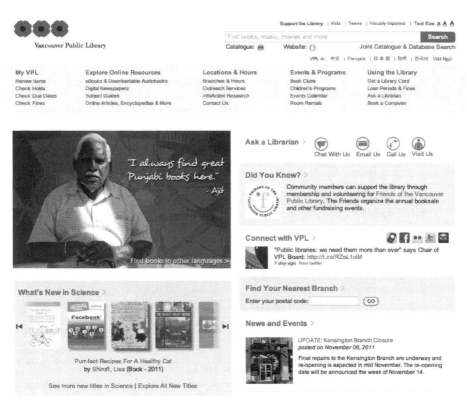

Figure 5.1A Vancouver (British Columbia) Public Library Web site

competing alternatives. The OPAC is still needed to provide access to the library's collections and provide necessary bibliographic control (although the evidence suggests that the richness and quality of the bibliographic record has never been appreciated, or used). Thus, the library catalog will continue to have declining value for library staff members and customers alike.

The online catalog has three discrete purposes:

1. It acts as a bibliographic database to materials housed in the library providing a number of indexes that an individual can search. The catalog may also provide links to other electronic resources, often materials not located within the library itself.

2. It performs as a portal providing links to nonbibliographic data (identifies the location and status of an item, identifies overdue materials, outstanding fines, allows customers to place a hold, update their patron record, and so forth).

3. It functions as a promotional artifact, advertising the presence of the library and the services it provides (Wells 2007).

Figure 5.1B Columbus (Ohio) Public Library Web site

Examining the standard reports available from a library's online catalog will reveal information about how frequently an index is used, how often a search will fail, the point at which a search is abandoned, and so forth.

Christine Borgman (1996) argued that the design of most online catalogs assumes that users formulate queries as a fixed goal and have complete knowledge about the author, title, or subject. Yet research has shown that users approach the catalog with incomplete information about any of the traditional access points, and thus online catalogs should be designed to answer questions instead of matching queries. Although vendors have been adding functionality for years, the fact remains that the online catalog has remained essentially unchanged since their inception. In a recent article, Karen Markey (2007) reviewed the reasons why the online catalog has fallen from grace:

- Searching the library online catalog puts people on an emotional roller coaster.

Figure 5.1C The Topeka & Shawnee County Public Library Online Catalog

- Translating information needs into words is difficult.

- Knowing what you want and where to look is important.

- Searching for something one does not know results in frenetic, aimless, and random activity.

Users of a Web-based online catalog can often move from screen to screen quite easily, and yet their actions can lead to the wrong conclusions. Another study found that users often conclude that when they do not find something, the library does not own the desired item. An observation study of four library online catalogs produced a total of 98 usability problems (White et al. 2006). These problems were sorted into six groups: layout (36 percent), ease of use (20 percent), functionality (17 percent), terminology (16 percent), feedback, and help.

Not surprisingly, the Internet is clearly having an impact on users from all types of libraries. Eric Novotny (2004) found novice users were impatient in choosing their type of search and in evaluating their search results. They assumed search results were sorted by relevance and thus did not frequently browse past the initial screen of results. Interestingly, more experienced users used more specific keyword terms and were more persistent in reviewing their search results and considering their options. No matter what type of search a task called for, participants tended to expect a simple keyword search to lead to optimal results presented in relevancy-ranked order (much like they experience when they use Google).

Susan Augustine and Courtney Greene (2002) measured the amount of time and number of clicks it took to perform a given task and compared these measures with those of an "expert." They found that users employ a trial-and-error method when searching online catalogs, are frequently unable to interpret the information they retrieve, and struggle to understand commonly used library jargon or terminology. Similar results were noted in another Web usability study (Brantley et al. 2006). OPACs must embrace an interface design that is redefined using new, Web-based standards of usability—ease of use rules the day (Fast and Campbell 2004).

Karen Markey and her colleagues (1999) examined end-user understanding of subject headings to determine the extent to which children and adults understood subdivided subject headings. A total of 48 children and 48 adults were recruited to participate in the study from three Michigan public libraries. The study found that about 36 percent of the meanings users gave to subject headings were correct. Context or subject heading order did not affect user understanding.

For almost every public library a keyword search is the dominant form of searching (Waller 2010). As shown in Figure 5.2, keyword searching is followed by title browse, and author browse. Note that Boolean searching typically accounts for less than 1 percent of all searches (and most of these searches are performed by reference librarians).

One of the consistent findings of numerous studies of the online catalog, despite improvements in the user interface and the display of results, a high proportion of users receive zero results for their searches (Ballard and Blaine 2011, Craven et al. 2010, Kress et al. 2011). The failure rates hover around 50 percent. Few users realize that the catalog has a controlled vocabulary, the arcane nature of subject headings eludes the majority of users, and the total experience of

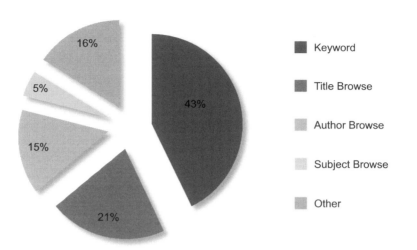

Figure 5.2. Type of Online Catalog Searches

using the OPAC is simply baffling. Given that many library customers use the catalog irregularly, it is not surprising that as little of 10 percent of the users entering the library actual use the online catalog.

As Lorcan Dempsey (2012) has observed, the catalog may give way to other environments that may employ catalog data so that while the catalog's functionality may disappear, the data itself is likely to be rebundled in a changing network discovery and workflow environments.

Next Generation Online Catalog

For several years, library vendors and the library community as a whole have been discussing exactly what features should be available in the "next generation online catalog." Hoffman and Yang (2011) developed a checklist of twelve "next generation catalog" features. These features, along with those noted by Laurel Tarulli (2012), include:

- Single point of entry for all resources—books, audio/visual materials, digital collections as well as pointers to articles in electronic journals

- State-of-the-art Web interface

- Enriched content—book cover images, descriptions, ratings, tagging (also know as folksonomy or collaborative tagging, social classification, social indexing, and social tagging), reviews

- Faceted navigation—allows the user to narrow a search by choosing a subject heading, date range, language, availability, and so forth

- Simple keyword search box—a link to an advanced search should also be provided

- Relevancy—more frequently circulated materials should be ranked higher

- Did you mean—spelling correction capabilities

- Recommendations to related materials

- User contributions—psummaries, reviews, comments, ratings, folksonomies

- RSS feeds

- Integration with social networking sites

- Provide an interface in multiple languages

- Persistent links

One of the important distinctions about the next generation catalog is that content flowing up from users is more valuable than the content flowing outward from the library to the customer. This means that the user should be able to add tags, a review, and comments to a posted review, and tags and comments to records contained in the library's online catalog. One of the real ironies is that libraries move so slowly to embrace Web 2.0 concepts—including the ability to build a community around books so that library users could add reviews, comments, ratings, and so forth—that sites such as *LibraryThing* now have cataloged almost 80 million books.

Of particular interest to libraries is that *LibraryThing* has developed a set of application programming interfaces (APIs) that enable a library to add a variety of addition content to its online catalog. *LibraryThing* provides access to almost two million reviews, more than 12 million ratings, and more than 92 million tags and can be easily added to a library's OPAC. A library can choose to include ratings and reviews, tag-based discovery, similar books, series, awards, visually browsing book covers in shelf list order, other editions, and Lexile measures that help find materials by reading levels. Library customers can contribute reviews (which are moderated by library staff members). The end result is a much larger and richer database that will significantly improve the user's OPAC experience. An analysis by one library found that about 50 percent of the *LibraryThing* tags already exist in the bibliographic record and almost half of the library's catalog records were enriched by using *LibraryThing* (Voorbij 2012). Additional resources that a library might want to consider integrating into the catalog content are from Goodreads and Shelfari.[1]

Among some of the next generation online catalog are: AquBrowser, BiblioCommons, Encore, Endeca, Primo, and vuFind (Nagy 2011A).

Yet, as noted by Eli Neiburger (2010), the ability for a library's customers to add content raises some significant privacy and security challenges that must be addressed by the library.

The impact that Google has had on everyone's perceptions about what a search does can't be overstated. This means that if your library OPAC or the databases that the library provides access to do not behave in the same way as Google, then the library has a real problem. Thus, the library needs to advocate with its vendors to ensure that these systems become more Google-like. So today libraries are confronted with the reality that many library OPACs and databases:

- Do not rank by relevance
- Do not do an implied AND when two or more words are included in a search request
- Do not do stemming by default (*walk* also finds *walks, walking, walked*)
- Will not drop search terms (to improve search results)
- Do not provide access to the full-text

Remember that in the end, the library customer wants an OPAC that:

- Looks like popular Web sites (read Google-like)
- Has enhanced information such as summaries, abstracts, table of contents, ratings, reviews, and other quality assessment information
- Leads directly to find needed information (users want to *find* while librarians like to *search* (OCLC 2009)

Web Discovery Systems

The early online catalogs provided access to a library's book collection. Over the course of time, additional material formats were added (audio tapes, video tapes, CD, DVD, manuscripts, and so forth) until the abyss of the Grand Canyon (journal articles, magazines, and newspaper articles) was encountered. And so for several decades the abyss has remained. One solution developed by the library automation vendors was called *federated search*. The idea was that the same search request was simultaneously sent to multiple sources, search engines, electronic journals, abstracting and indexing databases, and full-text databases. The federated search system often retrieved links to content found on other platforms. And these links were often old and the user often wound up getting lost in a confusing array of links. Then a tool was developed to resolve this problem, called a Link Resolver. A recent study by Breeding (2012) found that most libraries are satisfied with the performance of the Link Resolver in its effectiveness of connecting users to appropriate copies of electronic resources. I think it would be interesting to note that the libraries are satisfied and no study has been conducted to check on the satisfaction of federated searching from the customer's perspective.

However, in the last few years a new concept, called a Web-based Discover Service, has emerged so now it is possible to conceive of a unified catalog that provides access to all of the library's physical and electronic resources down to the article level. The intent is to provide access to the best quality information in a most convenient manner.

Web scale discovery can be considered a deep discovery tool within the vast ocean of content. Most of the commercially available options today provide access to a huge, centralized, pre-aggregated index that can be searched by the end user.

Web scale discovery services provide a range of services that have the following traits:

- **Content**. Content is created by harvesting local library resources (data from the online catalog), combined with publishers and aggregators allowing access to the full-text content for indexing purposes. Note that the library user only sees references (citations) to journal article content that has been licensed by the library.

- **Discovery**. A single box providing a Google like search experience is made available.

- **Delivery**. Results are ranked by relevancy offering options and design cues to improve the user's experience.

- **Flexibility**. The library has the opportunity to customize the services that will be most appealing to its community (Vaughn 2011).

There are five Web scale discover services. The first four services discussed below all create a pre-harvested, pre-aggregated central index. The services that are available include:

- Ebsco Discovery Services

- Ex Libris Primo Central

- OCLC WorldCat Local

- Serials Solutions Summon

- Innovative Interfaces Encore Synergy— It is interesting to note that Synergy does not create a pre-harvested, pre-aggregated central index.

Unfortunately, there is a real lack of transparency about the capabilities of each of these systems concerning both the breadth of content—that volume A of journal B is included in the discovery service—and depth of content—for journal C, metadata only is indexed, and for journal D, metadata and full text are indexed—which makes relying on the results of a discovery service such a sketchy proposition. You think you are performing a comprehensive search when in reality the search is deep in some areas and merely scratches the surface in others.

Implementation of a Web scale discovery service involves a lot of planning regarding what to include/exclude from the service, what to call (brand) the service on your library's Web site, how to download and transfer the library's records to the selected vendor, developing marketing plans, and so forth.

One library found that their users were downloading many more journal articles using the new Web scale discovery service—the increase ranged from 25 percent to more than 100 percent and the reaction of the users were quite positive. Users loved the single search box (Guajardo and Vacek 2012). Another study showed a dramatic decrease in the use of traditional online abstracting and indexing databases and a dramatic use of full-text resources (full-text databases and online journals) using the Web scale discovery service (Way 2010).

One alternative to a Web scale discovery service is to use Ezsearch (an advanced federated system used by a number of large academic (and some public) libraries.

However, let's be clear about a couple of points:

- Web scale discovery systems are not inexpensive and the library must pay an ongoing yearly fee to continue to use the service (in most libraries the Web scale discovery system actually replaces the library's online catalog).

- A Web scale discovery service has the potential, despite its imperfections (and there are always challenges with any system), to radically change the way users interact with the library's online systems to discover information resources. That is, the user discovers and uses more relevant material (both in the library and online) in the first few screens than is currently the case when they are required to use several systems [with their own unique user interface to learn].

The New York Public Library developed a statement, dubbed the Readers-First Initiative,[3] that outlines four principles libraries want e-content providers to follow that enables library users to:

- Search and browse a single comprehensive catalog with all of the library's offerings at once, including all eBooks, physical collections, blogs, and so forth. Currently, content providers often only allow searches within the products they sell, depriving users of the comprehensive library experience.

- Place holds, checkout items, view availability, manage fines, and receive communications within individual library catalogs or in the venue the library that will serve them best, without having to visit separate Web sites.

- Seamlessly enjoy a variety of eContent. To do this, libraries must be able to choose content, devices, and apps from any provider or from multiple vendors, without bundling that limits a library's ability to serve content they purchase on platforms of their choice.

- Download eBooks that are compatible with all eBook readers, from the Kindle to the Nook to the iPad and so forth. A new standard eBook format, EPUB 3, promises to do much to achieve this latter goal (Enis (B) 2013).

eResources

Libraries have been providing access to electronic books (eBooks) and electronic resources (electronic journals and an aggregation of electronic journals—sometimes called databases) for some time. The extent to which these electronic resources are used varies greatly, depending upon the resources that have been selected, what platforms they employ, and how easy it is to find these resources on a library's Web site.

The advantages of gaining access to electronic resources are obvious: any time, anywhere, any device has access to information. In short, there is no need to visit the physical library.

There are a variety of ways a library can gain access to eResources including:

- Purchase/own or lease eContent

- Pay-per-view (journal articles)

- Single-user or simultaneous multiple-user access

- Institutional or consortia purchase/licenses

- Aggregator, "Big Deal" or title-by-title access

- Full-text database, publisher eJournal collections, individual eJournals

- User demand-driven acquisitions or librarian-selected eContent.

Libraries, by and large, do little to market the availability and benefits of using electronic resources. For many, it is difficult to move away from the "library as place" marketing mindset. Aside from the obvious techniques of banners, posters, and bookmarks, libraries could be using email as a way to communicate with their customers about the benefits of using electronic resources. In addition, libraries might place an electronic display near the door of the library extoling the availability and benefits of electronic resources through the library's Web site.

One important project that bears watching is the Digital Public Library of America (DPLA) which went live April 19, 2013.[4] The DPLA, using open-source tools, is designed to complement a public library's offerings since users will increasingly rely on digital materials located in the cloud. The role of the library will continue to change from a warehouse for physical materials toward a vibrant community space that serves a variety of functions related to information. The DPLA is designed to accomplish three goals: create a well-organized portal of digital materials from national and regional libraries, archives, and museums to facilitate searching and browsing; provide metadata and digital tools that others can use to build new applications; and provide leadership to encourage open and collective access to the nation's shared cultural record.

Initially two apps are available for downloading by users (*Library Observatory* is an interactive tool for searching and visualizing the DPLA collections, accompanied by an interactive documentary that weaves together history, visualizations, and audio clips; and *Search DPLA and Europeana*, to discover digital resources in the United States and Europe). The user can search for items as well as browse using a map, a timeline, or explore an exhibition. The DPLA offers intriguing possibilities for a public library to broaden its reach to the ever-expanding world of digital resources. An application programming interface or API is available (the first of many I would hope) to foster integration and creativity.

Initially, the DPLA will provide access to the digital resources from seven state libraries as well as from seven large providers (Harvard University libraries, the Library of Congress, and others). DPLA provides access to photographs, manuscripts, books, newspapers, oral histories, other audio files, streaming video, and more.

eBooks

> *The library of tomorrow should be better than the library of today. The ability to loan our books to more than one person at once is a feature, not a bug.*
> —Cory Doctorow

The form of the book has changed over time and the most recent form is the eBook. Interestingly, some now call the print book a "pBook." The popularity of the eBook has increased as consumers are presented with more affordable options for "reading" an eBook. Amazon announced in 2011 that it had sold more eBooks than pBooks for the first time in its history. Sales of eBooks in the U.S. in 2011 amounted to more than $169 million (AAP 2011). In addition to the growing number of eBooks from commercial publishers, more than a million eBooks are available at little or no cost from self-publishers (seemingly the vanity press knows no bounds). According to a recent Pew Center Research report, 21 percent of American adults read an eBook in the last year, 68 percent read a pBook, while 19 percent read no books (Purcell 2012). Tablet owners and eReader owners report that they read more (eBooks and pBooks) since the advent of the eBook (Zickuhr 2012).

eReaders

A dedicated eReader is a device that is optimized for reading eBooks—the Kindle, Nook, Kobo, and Sony Reader are among the more popular eReaders available. The cost of eReaders has declined significantly and is likely that prices will go even lower. What is special about an eReader is that it is a light device with a fairly long battery life that will store thousands of eBooks. The eReader uses a technology called E-Ink that has no backlighting so it is easier on the eyes and can be used outdoors. eBooks can be downloaded from many sites using wireless technology.

A non-dedicated eReader is a device designed for some other larger purpose that can also read ePublications (eBooks, eMagazines, electronic journal articles, and so forth). Examples of a non-dedicated eReader include the PC, Mac, iPad, iPhone, Android phones/tablets, TVs, and so forth. Interesting, 2012 may have been the year when the most eReaders were sold as many sales forecasts suggest that eReader sales will be slowing in 2013.

An alphabet soup of electronic "document" formats can be downloaded (AZW, PDF, EPUB, MOBI, TXT, DJVU, LIT, etc.); the most popular are EPUB, PDF, and AZW (Kindle). In the ideal world, any eReader or non-dedicated eReader would be able to receive, store, and display any document format. But, as you know, we do not live in an ideal world. Some vendors, for obvious competitive reasons, will only support one or two electronic document formats— often the formats that are proprietary and thus lock customers in to their eReader.

In addition to competing formats, we also have dueling DRMs (Digital Rights Management). DRM is a software "lock" that controls access to a file and the user needs the correct software "key" to unlock it. Some simply ignore the DRM while others take it as a personal challenge to "unlock" the DRM lock and then share the digital file with their friends.

eBooks have obvious benefits for all libraries. There is no need to provide physical space for eBooks and the costly, polluting, labor intensive process of moving pBooks from one branch to another is eliminated (PinpointLogic 2010, OECD 2012). The library's Web site becomes "the" library and it allows customers to visit the library anywhere, anytime to place reserves and download eBooks. Overdue notices are no longer needed as the book "self-returns" when due. Yet, as the prices for eBooks continue to rise (at least for libraries) coupled with the cost of providing a technology component (in some cases), the overall costs for a library to provide access to eBooks may exceed the costs of acquiring print books.

A 2011 survey conducted for *Library Journal* (2011) found that about 72 percent of all public libraries provide access to eBooks—this number has increased to almost nine out of ten libraries in 2012 (*Library Journal* 2012). The survey also found that the libraries provided to their patrons an average of more than 1,500 fiction and nonfiction eBooks. Thanks to Google Books, Project Gutenberg, the Internet Archive, and others, more than a million eBooks can be downloaded for free. The Internet Archive has a new *Digital Lending Library* that should be of interest to every public library hosted on OpenLibrary.Org.

Purchasing/Licensing Options

In almost all cases, a library does not purchase an eBook but rather it is buying content in a container that includes software, a license agreement, DRM, and an ongoing relationship with a vendor. Generally the content a library wants will determine the vendor(s), a business model, license, and format the library will get. This is particularly true for public libraries, which have limited choices for purchasing best-selling fiction. As can be seen in Figure 5.3, there is a wide

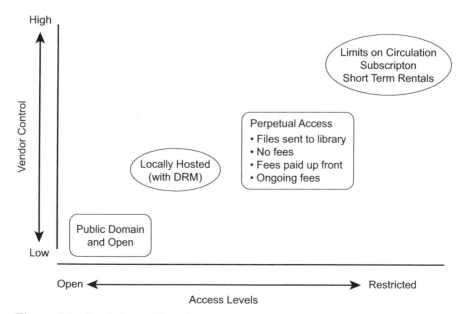

Figure 5.3. eBook Access Levels

range of access options (from open to very restricted) and as vendors assume more control, more restrictions are placed on a library. In addition, as vendor restrictions increase the risk for ongoing access, content also increases.

Acquiring eBooks

There are a number of options available for people to download free eBooks as noted in the adjoining sidebar. One of the most popular sites is the Internet Archive, which provides access to more than two million eBooks that are out of copyright (this site experiences more than ten million downloads per month!).

Free eBook Sites

Internet Archive	DailyLit
Google Books	HathiTrust
Big Universe	Book Glutton
Free Literature	Children's Books Online
Children's Literature Bookshelf	Many Books
Classic Reader	Fiction.us
Scribd	World Public Library
Magic Keys	FeedBooks
Free-eBooks.net	HundredZeros
BookBub	Free Par-TAY
FreeBooksy	OpenLibrary

Libraries can purchase or license eBooks directly from a publisher or an aggregator. Among those of interest for public libraries are OverDrive (the leader among public libraries), EBSCOhost (or netLibrary), Ebrary, Ingram's MyiLibrary, Books 24x7, 3M, Baker & Taylor's Axis 360, and Freading.

It is interesting to compare the best-selling eBooks from Amazon, Barnes and Noble, and Smashwords (a Web site that helps author's self-publish their books) as shown in Table 5.2. An interesting exercise for a library is to determine what proportions of the best selling eBooks are accessible to your library's customers. Does your library have any eBooks distributed by Smashwords or other self-publishers in the library catalog? Given that there are many more self-published eBooks than pBooks "published" each year, public libraries have only begun to scratch the surface in providing access to this ever increasingly popular way of producing eBooks. Interestingly, Smashwords has launched a new service, Library Direct, which allows a library to purchase large collections of Smashwords eBooks—depending on the number of eBooks purchased, the price can be as low as four dollars per eBook.

Table 5.2. Top 10 eBook Best Sellers in 2012

Amazon	Barnes & Noble	Smashwords
Fifty Shades Freed	Submerged	Bēn Thăng Cuô
The Hunger Games	The Reason	Our Universal Journey
Catching Fire	Safe Haven	Incendiary
Mockingjay	A Rake's Vow	Spinward Fringe Broadcast
Gone Girl	Gone Girl	Offshore Apocalypse
The Hunger Games Trilogy	Release Me	Soap Opera Uncensored #57
Bared to You	The Coincidence of Callie & Kayden	The Duchess War
The Racketeer	Someone to Love	Rothschild Guide to Football Handicapping
Reflected in You	Fifty Shades Darker	Soap Opera Uncensored #58
The Lucky One	Fifty Shades of Gray	Wisdom

There are many hindrances to libraries purchasing self-published works, including the fact that they are legion, the quality varies wildly, and that legitimate, informative reviews are scarce. These obstacles can be overcome with approaches like that being pursued by the Douglas County (CO) Public Library, and may even dissolve over time as vetting services arise.

eBook Platforms

Providing access to eBooks in a library setting requires a platform that provides access to an attractive catalog and the necessary technical infrastructure. The eBook platform aggregates user data; tracks preferences; integrates social information; and allows users to rate an item, write a review, and so forth. The eBook platform can be provided by a vendor or the library can manage its own platform as suggested by James LaRue, driector of the Douglas County (CO) Library (2012). 3M has used the platform created by Douglas County as the basis for their eBook platform.

The eBook platform developed by the Douglas County Library (Sendze 2012) is one that most public libraries would be able to duplicate and includes the following components:

- A hardware server
- Adobe Content Server software for DRM-protected software
- VuFind (open source) discovery front end
- An online eReader for all eBook content
- Software to control the downloading and lending of eBooks
- A large screen power wall visual display (as well as a mobile app) to raise the visibility of eBooks in the library
- A link to purchase eBook content if the desired eBook is not available from the library.

eBook Challenges

However, several important issues arise as libraries, vendors, and publishers struggle to define how eBooks will be provided to a library and their customers. Among these issues are:

- Does the library own the eBook? Some vendors and publishers are only licensing the right to use an eBook (for a period of time or for a specific number of uses, after which, the library must purchase another license for a specific number of uses).
- Moving from one vendor to another means, in most cases, that the licensed content is lost and must be licensed again.
- Some libraries have decided to skip the purchase of HarperCollins eBook titles in the wake of the publisher's decision to set a license limit of 26 checkouts per title. Should your library follow a similar path?
- Some of the major publishers have decided not to license eBooks to any library (this is called disintermediation) and rely on direct sales to the end user.
- Recently HarperCollins decided to double or triple its eBook prices to libraries (without adding any other value). Should a library do business with a publisher that is price gouging?
- Not every owner of an eReader has the financial means to purchase every eBook they wish to read. Yet the major publishers are only focused on individual sales and are not interested in making sales to libraries. A recent study found that over 50 percent of all library users report purchasing books (and eBooks) by an author they were introduced to in the library (Albanese 2011).

- Should the same set of policies that apply to pBooks also apply to eBooks? Must an item be returned to the library before it can be borrowed again? Can (should) an eBook be loaned simultaneously to two or more customers?

- Can the library download an eBook to its own (or consortium) server or is the eBook only accessible if the library patron visits the vendor's Web site (such as with OverDrive, 3M, Ingram, or Baker & Taylor)?

- Should the library purchase eReaders to loan to its customers? If yes, should a single type or brand of eReader be selected or should the customer have several options (the answer has obvious budget implications)?

- Is the complexity of the process to download an eBook too much that it turns off the library customer so that the library no longer is a viable option?

- Is staff sufficiently trained to respond to a wide variety of questions pertaining to the set up, downloading, and use of several eReaders?

- Amazon's Kindle Owner's Lending Library bears careful watching by librarians as some observers suggest this is a real threat to libraries lending eBooks. That is, for a very low monthly fee, people can download eBooks from Amazon for an unlimited time period.

- What is the library's legal liability if a patron defeats the DRM software lock and stores a copy of the eBook on their own personal computer or a handheld digital device?

- Should a library also offer access to the pay-per-use or metering model offered by some vendors such as Freading?

- Some librarians have suggested that the publisher should publish and the library should own, lend, and preserve the content (which implies being able to store, lend, and preserve access to eBooks and other electronic content).

- And at least two observers have suggested that libraries get out of the eBook business altogether (Newman 2012). Sarah Houghton (2012) has suggested that librarians haven't been heard largely because we've been too polite and too quiet too long. It's our fault. We removed ourselves from the equation by not being more proactive as a profession through the professional organizations and lobbyists we expect to speak for us. But even now that some of us are getting louder and angrier, we're still being ignored by the entire eBooks industry, with very few exceptions.

eBooks are changing the game for publishers as well as for vendors and librarians. The uncertainty of the marketplace means that the future of providing access to eBooks is cloudy and uncertain. Nobody really knows the full range of opportunities and threats that eBooks bring to the table. Thus, librarians need to be more proactive about the ways in which their public libraries will provide access to eBooks (O'Brien et al. 2012).

Frustrated with all of the various restrictions confronting librarians and library eBook users, Sarah Houghton has suggested an "eBook User's Bill of Rights" (2011):

Every eBook user should have the following rights:

- The right to use eBooks under guidelines that favor access over proprietary limitations

- The right to access eBooks on any technological platform, including the hardware and software the user chooses

- The right to annotate, quote passages, print, and share eBook content within the spirit of fair use and copyright

- The right of the first-sale doctrine extended to digital content, allowing the eBook owner the right to retain, archive, share, and re-sell purchased eBooks

I believe in the free market of information and ideas.

I believe that authors, writers, and publishers can flourish when their works are readily available on the widest range of media. I believe that authors, writers, and publishers can thrive when readers are given the maximum amount of freedom to access, annotate, and share with other readers, helping this content find new audiences and markets. I believe that eBook purchasers should enjoy the rights of the first-sale doctrine because eBooks are part of the greater cultural cornerstone of literacy, education, and information access.

Digital Rights Management (DRM), like a tariff, acts as a mechanism to inhibit this free exchange of ideas, literature, and information. Likewise, the current licensing arrangements mean that readers never possess ultimate control over their own personal reading material. These are not acceptable conditions for eBooks.

I am a reader. As a customer, I am entitled to be treated with respect and not as a potential criminal. As a consumer, I am entitled to make my own decisions about the eBooks that I buy or borrow.

I am concerned about the future of access to literature and information in eBooks. I ask readers, authors, publishers, retailers, librarians, software developers, and device manufacturers to support these eBook users' rights.

These rights are yours. Now it is your turn to take a stand.

The one thing that is quite clear is that more and more people will demand access to eBooks (while sales of eReaders continue to be high people are beginning to move to tablets [with an eBook app]). The question to be answered by each library, will my public library play a role in providing access to eBooks for its customers?

A recent Pew Research Report (Zickuhr et al. 2012) noted that library cardholders use more technology, read more, and are more than twice as likely to have purchased their most recent book than borrowed it from the library. And almost half of customers who have previously borrowed an eBook from the library will have purchased their most recent eBook. However, a more recent Pew Research Report (Zickuhr et al. 2013) found that more than half of all Americans are unaware that public libraries provide access to eBooks.

Eli Neiburger, Associate Director of the Ann Arbor (MI) District Library, gave a provocative talk during the *Library Journal/School Library Journal* virtual conference on Ebooks: Libraries at the Tipping Point (September 2010). The "official" title of Eli's presentation was *Libraries at the Tipping Point: How eBooks Impact Libraries*. The "unofficial" title was *Libraries Are So Screwed*.[5]

In summary, Eli's thesis is the following:

Libraries are screwed, because we are invested in the codex, and the codex has become outmoded. It's not just a change of text delivery format, it's a move away from content that is ownable and shareable, and that's a problem when your organization is in the business of owning and sharing content.

The brand of libraries is the book temple. Come to the book temple and get yourself some books. Avid library users know that there's more to it, but . . . our values and our operation parameters and even our physical facilities are all built around the codex. If the eBook is the future of text distribution, then we're really screwed, because we are unlikely to ever have the access to these markets and the flexibility with our purchases that we currently have with the codex market.

The real problem is that the value of library collections is rooted in the worth of a local copy. The localness of something loses most of its embodied value when you can retrieve information from Australia in 300 milliseconds. Who cares if it's local or not? I have it immediately. The notion of a copy loses most of its embodied value when there's no longer a difference between transmission and duplication. When you're dealing with digital objects, to transmit it is to duplicate it. If you know where it is, you'll always have it. There are already more cell phones in the world than there are toilets, and in this century most humans are going to have persistent Internet access in their pocket. In an inter-networked world, when you can download anything from anywhere, the idea of having a local copy only makes sense to a hoarder.

There may not always be new material made available in formats that libraries can purchase. This has already started—we had our first request this past week for an item that is not available in print, it's only available on the Kindle. There's no way that we can buy it.

No digital native is going to get excited about waiting to receive a digital object, and what's the sense in making someone give something back to you when you still have it even after you gave it to them? Finally, the user experiences available to people who choose not to bother trying to use the library will only provide increasingly appealing value, which puts us in the situation where all this is happening as taxpayers are having to decide what municipal services they can live without. We are so screwed.

eBooks also open up another interesting "can of worms." That is, it is possible to embed software in an eReader or eBook app that tracks how the reader interacts with the eBook. Is the book read "cover to cover" (as most people do when reading fiction) for both fiction and nonfiction? What parts of an eBook are read and skipped? Do readers click on links (and which links are used)? How much time is spent reading? All of this data is stored and analyzed (certainly all of the aggregate data is analyzed but is an individual's data also analyzed?). How could (should) libraries use such intensive usage data to benefit their customers? Should libraries be concerned about individual privacy concerns when the retail customer has waived their rights when they download an eBook?

Another sobering reality is that the definition of what constitutes an eBook is constantly evolving. At what point does an eBook cease to be an eBook and be called something else. When the text of an eBook is combined with a series of videos, images, and audio files, as well as being able to link to Internet-based content, is it still an eBook? Is an eBook still an eBook when the content is automatically updated? When it carries advertising? Does it make sense to continue to divide up the world using old formats? Clearly digital text, audio, video, and other content is merging into something new. All of this makes for some thought-provoking discussions (if we can avoid the headaches).

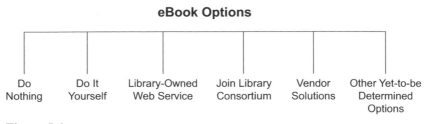

Figure 5.4.

So the available eBook options for a public library at this point would seem to be fairly limited as shown in Figure 5.4.

A related problem is that there is no easy way for a library to discover the diamonds from the lumps of coal among the hundreds of thousands of self-published eBooks from hundreds of Internet-based print-on-demand companies. And while Web sites such as Goodreads and Indie Reader (of course Amazon has reviews and recommends self-published eBooks published on their platform) provide some assistance it is necessary to visit several sites to begin the process of selecting eBooks for the library. While the library could encourage their customers to recommend eBooks to purchase, this approach still will reveal little when the need to discover good eBooks is so large. And the whole field of reviews of self-published eBooks is further complicated since there are a number of firms that will create favorable reviews (for a fee). David Vinjamuri (2013) has suggested that there is an opportunity for libraries to create a cooperative eBook recommendation system at the network level that would serve all libraries. Perhaps ALA will step up to the plate? Then again, perhaps not.

Library Association Efforts

Hoping to improve the eBook conversation between libraries and publishers, the American Library Association recently released two reports "eBook Business Models for Public Libraries" (ALA 2012) and "eBooks and Libraries: An Economic Perspective" (Besen and Kirby 2012). And the International Federation of Library Associations (IFLA) has recently released its "Principles for Library eLending" based on the assumption that it is:

> necessary for libraries and publishers/authors to negotiate a range of reasonable terms and conditions for the licensing of eBooks to library which allows them to fulfill their mission of guaranteeing access to knowledge and information for their communities. (IFLA 2013)

The assumption made by IFLA is an important one given the evidence that some publishers seem to be intent on cutting out libraries all together and relying solely on direct sales/licensing of eBooks to the customer.

eBook Resources

Given the dynamic and rapidly changing nature of the eBook landscape, some resources are suggested to assist you in keeping up. One particularly good resource is an ALA sponsored Webinar presented by Sue Polanka.[6]

Librarians that are arguing and lobbying for clever eBook lending solutions are completely missing the point. They are defending library as warehouse as opposed to fighting for the future, which is librarian as producer, concierge, connector, teacher and impresario. Post-Gutenberg, books are finally abundant, hardly scare, hardly expensive, hardly worth warehousing. Post-Gutenberg, the scarce resource is knowledge and insight, not access to data.
—Seth Godin (2011)

---

eBook Resources

No Shelf Required — www.noshelfrequired.com

LJ/SLJ ebook blog– www.thedigitalshift.com

ALA eContent blog- americanlibrariesmagazine.org/e-content

ALA TechSource blog — www.alatechsource.org/blog

Teleread — www.teleread.org

INFOdocket– www.infodocket.com

eBooknewser — www.mediabistro.com/ebooknewser/

The Digital Reader — www.the-digital-reader.com/

Go-to-hellman — go-to-hellman.blogspot.com

Apps

A mobile application or app is a software application or tool designed to run on smartphones, tablet computers, and other mobile devices. Individuals can download an app from a pool of more than seven hundred thousand apps (for free or by paying a small fee) from such providers as the Apple App Store, Google Play, Windows Phone Store, the Blackberry App World, or directly from an organization, including some public libraries. Apps perform a wide variety of tasks including email, stock market and weather information, GPS and location-based services, banking, playing orders for goods and services, and playing games (my grandkids love playing *Angry Birds*). In 2012, the usage of apps exceeded the usage of Web browsers on smartphones and tablets for the first time (Enis 2013).

Most library apps provide access to the library's catalog or special collections (the British Library Nineteenth Century Collection and the New York Public Library's Biblion World Fair). Some libraries, for example the District of Columbia Public Library, allow other libraries to download their open source apps for free. Your library can then easily modify the app and make it your own. As the world's population increasingly uses mobile phones for almost everything, every public library needs to be connected using apps.

Some libraries, for example the Darien (CT) Library and the Watertown (MA) Free Public Library, use iPads and an app to complement traditional story times with a digital story time activity that encourages children to physically participate in a story (Samtani 2012). Yet serious questions remain about the effectiveness and desirability of using electronic picture books with preschool and elementary school children. Given that many children are not reading at grade level, perhaps the exposure to ePicture books can be beneficial. However, some preliminary results suggest that the combination of print and eBooks is beneficial. One group of students using Tumblebooks, a provider of children's eBooks, was 23 percentage points higher in reading levels than a control group (Guernsey 2011). The study noted that the children had gained confidence and self-esteem in their reading skills.

Summary of Findings

Every public library today is really two libraries—the physical library and the virtual library. In this chapter we have learned that the public library must have more than a simple presence on the Internet. Its Web site must be visually appealing and refreshed frequently so that its content has value and meaning to those who wish to visit their public library "virtually." All of the available evidence suggests that ease of use and new content will keep people coming back time after time. Your library cannot afford to be "stuck" with an old Web site that turns people off. Your customers, both visible and invisible, must have a great customer experience so that they continue to use the library and its services as well as sharing their enthusiasm with others! This is the mark of a great library.

Take Action

A library should take a number of actions to improve the experience of using the virtual library. Among these are:

Library Web site

- Review the usability of your library's Web site and make a list of needed improvements

- Determine how much library jargon is currently being used on your library's Web site and replace the jargon with words and phrases more easily understood by people as noted in Table 5.1

- Make the library Web site more focused on meeting the needs of the customer

- Make the electronic resources more visible. Explain the use of each electronic resource as the primary way of organizing the databases (this means not in alphabetical order)

Online Catalog

- Generate a series of reports to determine how the catalog is currently being used—keyword, author, title, subject searches

- Determine how many searches retrieve no records (how many of these searches are for misspelled words?)

- What are the most popular searches (most frequently occurring)?

- Consider partnering with *LibraryThing* to provide additional content (ratings, reviews, covers, and other content) to your existing online catalog

- Explore the use of a next generation online catalog

- Would the use of a Web scale discovery system make sense for your library? What are the one-time and annual recurring ongoing costs of such a system for your library?

eResources

- Are there any electronic resources that the library should be using that it is not currently using?

- Is there a statewide or other available consortium that a library could join in order to reduce the costs of licensing electronic resources?
- Calculate a cost per use for each electronic resource. If the cost exceeds one dollar per use, consider other options for providing access to the desired resource (per article fee using document delivery and so forth)

eBooks

- Review the options for obtaining eBooks for your library. Is it possible to use another option that would provide comparable services (a different vendor, join a consortium, purchase rather than license eBooks, build your own eBook platform along the lines of Douglas County, CO, and so forth)
- Identify a way to identify self-published eBooks that the library should obtain

Apps

- Ask a staff member to identify open source apps that can be obtained from other libraries so that your library can provide apps to your customers.

Notes

1. Adapted from a Web site maintained by John Kupersmith. He also provides a citation for each study included in his chart. Available at http://www.jkup.net/terms-studies.html.

2. An interesting aside, Amazon.com owns Shelfari and Goodreads and has a 40 percent stake in *LibraryThing*. It would not be surprising to see one or more of these services combined into one service.

3. See www.readersfirst.org for more information.

4. For more information about the DPLA, visit http://dp.la/

5. You can listen to Eli's presentation at YouTube http://www.youtube .com/watch?v=KqAwj5ssU2c&feature=player_embedded

    You can download Eli's PowerPoint presentation at http://www.slideshare.net/we2aam/ebooks-impact

6. Sue Polanka's slides can be downloaded from Slideshare (http:// www.slideshare.net/ALATechSource/2013-ala-purchasing).

Selection Policies

What do most people care about? Public safety, employment, housing, and education—and the library speaks to all of those needs.

Crime? Libraries are a sanctuary for at-risk kids, on the loose after school lets out.

Employment? Libraries offer help wanted ads and books and programming on job-hunting, résumé writing, computer literacy, and ESL.

Housing? Libraries provide books and workshops on home remodeling, the home buying process, and financial planning.

Education? Librarians teach children to love reading, provide homework help, and offer guidance on college planning, SATs, and financial aid.

—Jose Aponte

The challenge confronting any library, including public libraries, is the continuing tension that exists due to the reality that the amount of materials published each year greatly exceeds what any one library or a group of libraries can realistically purchase. This tension is further exacerbated by the fact that the library must purchase most of the materials without knowing how well these selections will be received. Will the materials being added to the library's collection result in use? Will the library's customers find value in the library's collection?

Public libraries also face the difficulty of attempting to service the demand for highly popular items (e.g., books and other items on best seller lists), while recognizing that the demand will be fleeting only to be replaced by the demand for other newer popular materials. In public library circles, meeting this demand with a large number of multiple copies has been characterized by the saying "give 'em what they want." The counterpoint to this view has also been characterized by the practice that the library should purchase quality materials that patrons "should" or will want in years to come.

Interestingly, evidence of this tension has been around for more than a century. Consider that "the voracious devouring of fiction commonly indulged in by patrons of the public library, especially the young, is extremely pernicious and mentally unwholesome" (Lane 1899).

Another interesting tension occurs between those who wish to collect as much as possible and those who advocate for collecting only the "best"— however "best" is to be defined. In years past, as budgets would allow, in a paper-centric world collecting more materials was deemed a good strategy. This "more is better" strategy has been characterized as a "just-in-case" approach to collection development. While others have felt that the best course of action was responding to the needs of the customers with a "just-in-time" approach.

Yet, as seen in Figure 6.1, the majority of materials the library purchased are increasingly becoming available from a number of competition sources as was discussed in chapter one. Thus, the value of the local library's collection is rapidly declining. What has real value now, and for the foreseeable future, are the library's special collections, especially its materials that have historical significance. We are living in a world that is moving from local to global, from linear to linked, and from print to digital.

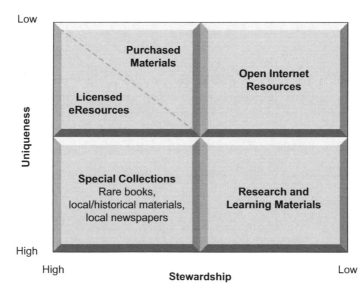

Figure 6.1. Collection Grid

Collection Development Plan/Policy

All libraries periodically go through a planning process. Planning assists a library in focusing on goals along with the objectives or steps to reach those goals. A good planning process will also develop performance measures to assist in determining if those goals are being reached. The development and refreshing of a collection development plan is a natural extension of the library planning process.

A written collection development policy can also be called selection policies, collection statements, or collection development plans. Whatever the document is called, it provides a plan for building and maintaining a collection—be they physical or digital materials. The plan provides a basis for selection and deselection and establishes priorities for the library and librarians as well as establishing policies concerning gifts and exchange of materials. The plan sets out principles to be followed for turning policy into action. The collection development policy assists the library in dealing with individuals who question why some materials are selected and others are ignored.

A good collection development policy has several characteristics:

- It is written.
- It provides a framework and parameters but is not too detailed.
- It is designed to inform as well as to protect.
- There is room for flexibility while striving for consistency.
- It is periodically reviewed and revised as needed.

The principal value of a collection development policy is that it serves as a vehicle for communication with the library's management team, staff members, and outside constituencies. The policy allows the library management team to ensure consistency and control over the additions to the collection, even in the face of selectors who may be distributed geographically. A library's collection development policy can also be used to document and support cooperative collection development activities with other libraries.

A collection development policy is also effective in assisting the library to protect itself from external pressures by protecting intellectual freedom and helps prevent censorship. Many library collection development policies refer to the American Library Association's Library Bill of Rights and other statements of intellectual freedom. The policy may include specific procedures for handling a complaint against materials currently in the library's collection. With procedures in place, it helps ensure that challenged materials will be fairly reviewed. The pressures from the outside can also run the other way, in that the library may be asked to include certain materials that may be inappropriate. A policy thus makes it clear that materials are rejected due to collection guidelines, and not the individual librarian who is making the determination.

Aligning the Budget

Some public libraries have established goals for what percent of the library's budget should be devoted to the acquisitions budget. For some libraries, the goal can be as high as 20 percent while for many the library's acquisitions budget rarely rises above 8 to 10 percent. And in this time of financial pressures on library budgets (for many libraries the pressure will actually mean a budget reduction from 20 to 40 percent or more), the first place that library boards and library directors often choose is to reduce the acquisition's budget.

And yet, as noted in earlier chapters, one of the compelling reasons for many people to choose to visit the public library is that they will find the "new stuff." Thus, if the collection becomes dated over time as the acquisition's budget is cut and then cut again, the amount of new materials that can be purchased will obviously decline.

The majority of public libraries allocate the acquisition's budget in direct proportion to the amount of use the various types of materials receive. This is clearly the most equitable manner in which to allocate the acquisition's budget.

Loan Policies and Duplicates

Libraries have long struggled to find the right balance between the number of copies needed (and the real costs associated with purchasing additional copies) and the length of time people have to wait for a copy of a desired item. Customer satisfaction is noticably improved when the title availability rates improve. Customers fail to find a desired title due primarily to its being already checked out by another customer. This is another manifestation of the 80/20 rule—that is, 80 percent or more of circulation comes from a very small percent of the library's total collection—20 percent or less (Britten 1990, Trueswell 1969).

As noted by Michael Buckland (1975), three major factors influence the availability rates for desired items:

- The number of copies owned by the library
- The length of the loan period
- The level of customer demand for the item

The level of customer demand is clearly outside the control of the library (although the library can anticipate some of the likely demand). Thus, the library can mitigate to some extent whether the customer finds the desired item on the shelf and available for borrowing.

Duplicate Copies

Library staff members have been reluctant to duplicate popular items for fear that these popular materials would consume a large portion of their materials acquisition's budget. Yet, there is plentiful evidence that when multiple copies are purchased, these duplicate copies account for a small portion of the overall budget. Staff is also hesitant to purchase multiple copies for fear that the demand for popular materials will fall off rapidly and that the multiple copies will sit idle on the shelf. In reality, an item that circulates 15 times in the space of a year provides the same level of value to the customer as a title that circulates 15 times over the space of five years. When low-circulating items are weeded (including multiple copies of the same title) they can be donated to a library Friends group for sale, sold online, or donated to other organizations within the community.

Some libraries have found that leasing popular materials (a number of leasing programs are available from several library vendors) is a more reasonable approach and it removes the need for the library to dispose of no-longer circulating materials (these items are simple returned to the leasing vendor).

Whatever the approach, public libraries continually face the inevitable dilemma of "giving them what they want" (popularized by the Baltimore County Public Library under the leadership of Charlie Robinson) versus building a collection of what they should read. Most library selectors consider a number of factors when deciding to purchase multiple copies: amount of use of other titles by the same author, genre, subject matter, format, planned promotional budget, and so forth. One small library in New Hampshire emulated the Baltimore County approach and provides multiple copies of the best sellers and found that their budgets increased significantly over a five-year period (Sullivan 2000).

Varying the Loan Period

Shortening the loan period increases the availability rate for popular materials. Yet, this also creates a tension in the mind of the customer, as they may want to keep the item longer than they are allowed to due to the checkout period. While it is possible to consider shortening the loan periods for all items in the library's collection, in reality most libraries use shorter loan periods for popular materials including:

- *Popular formats* such as DVDs (three-day, five-day, or one-week loan periods), audio books for two weeks, and most books for four weeks.

- *Popular titles*—could have shorter loan periods. Such materials might be titles on the best seller list, newer mysteries, diet and cooking books, newer DIY books, and computer manuals.
- *Seasonal demand*—for selected materials (Valentine's Day, President's Day, Fourth of July, Halloween, Thanksgiving, Christmas, and so forth) can be more equitably met with shorter loan periods.
- *Popular authors*—may necessitate a shorter loan period. For example, all of J.K. Rowling's *Harry Potter* books as well as Stephanie Meyer's *Twilight* series required a short loan period.
- *Deadline looming*—may require a short loan period of specific titles that have been assigned by a teacher for a specific project.

The Balancing Act

Achieving the correct balancing act between purchasing multiple copies of popular materials versus shortening the loan periods for such items is something that each library will have to determine over time. The reality is that your library will find the correct balancing point if it considers three tenets:

- *Align the materials acquisition's budget* with the goals established for the library. If the library has selected a goal of meeting the demand for current topics and titles then more of the acquisition's budget would likely be spent on purchasing duplicate copies of popular materials. However, if the library has established a goal of encouraging lifelong learning, then more of its budget would likely be spent on acquiring a broader range of titles (with a corresponding requirement to meet less of the demand for popular materials).
- *Acknowledge the interrelationship of duplication and shortened loan periods* to improve the availability of the desired items. Incumbent in this tenet is the requirement to continuously monitor the availability rates being experienced by the library's customers and making adjustments as needed.
- *Focus on the needs of the community served by a library location* rather than on the broader community. People will only travel relatively short distances to visit the physical library so ensuring that the materials in the library will meet their local needs is much more important than focusing on the all-encompassing community-wide needs.

Public libraries will for some time to come continue to focus on providing access to physical materials (books, DVDs, CDs, and so forth), which is not true for academic libraries (who spend a vast majority of their acquisition's budget on electronic journals and databases). Yet, the trend to digital content is irreversible, especially in the face of Google's continuing efforts to digitize library books. So, a part of the library's balancing act is to ensure that it does provide access to a suite of electronic resources that meets the needs of its community and monitors how much these resources are being used.

Selecting Materials

Let's be up-front about the actual costs associated with the selection and ordering of materials—it's expensive! Staff time plus the actual costs for the materials themselves means that the costs of selecting, ordering, receiving, cataloging, and processing of materials for a library's collection is a major expense. Not surprisingly, there are several approaches that a library can choose. These approaches include:

- *Centralized.* A centralized approach may mean a single individual or a group of people are responsible for the selection and ordering of materials. As the size of the library increases the more likely it is to find a centralized unit responsible for the selection and ordering of materials. The unit may be responsible for the selection of all materials or only for a subset. Typically a centralized unit is responsive to suggestions from other staff members and particularly responsive to requests received directly from the customer. While the selection of titles from established and published lists is fairly straightforward, some libraries also create and maintain a list of items being considered for selection.

   The obvious advantage of a centralize selection process is that it reduces costs by reducing the number of people involved in the selection process (Irvine 1995). In a centralized selection unit, the professional librarian should be spending their time assessing the results of the selection process by immersing themselves in the usage reports that can be quickly generated using the integrated library system (ILS). Selection decisions that result in materials not being used must be reexamined so such decisions are not allowed to continue.

   Typically, a centralized unit performs four functions:

   ° *Consider items* that might be added to a library's collection. The library might maintain a list of items being considered for selection or maintain a consideration list using a vendor's system.

   ° *Select items* in a wide variety of formats to meet the needs of the library and the community that it serves. In addition to the obvious best sellers and award-winning titles that will be of interest, a wide variety of other titles must be considered and some selections made. A centralized unit can also help ensure that high demand items are purchased and processed quickly helping to guarantee the availability of popular items.

○ *Purchase materials* from an appropriate source. In addition to the traditional library vendors such as Baker & Taylor, Ingram Books, and other suppliers are available online that can provide materials quickly and at affordable rates.

Most libraries have developed formulas and rules of thumb when considering the number of copies to order. Among the factors that are usually considered are:

- The popularity of the author or creator

- The popularity of the genre or subject area

- The established service goals and objectives for the library

- The duplication and loan periods

- The presence (and extent) of the holds queue

- The format

- The cost

While some libraries with branches allocate an equal number of each title to each branch, other libraries allocate according to historical use data (DVDs move slowly in one branch and rapidly in another), or according to the intended use of the branch library (Family/early literacy, a research branch, and so forth).

○ *Process materials* that have been received from a supplier. While some libraries have embraced the outsourcing of the cataloging and processing of all ordered materials to their suppliers, other libraries continue to rely on staff to perform this activity. Every library should carefully assess how its technical services unit adds real value to its activities. And value needs to be defined from the customer's perspective rather than relying on the fact that traditionally libraries have always performed these "backroom" activities.

- *Decentralized.* A decentralized approach assigns the selection responsibility for a particular area of the collection to a number of staff members. Each staff member is provided a budget and makes selections in their subject area over the course of the year. These subject area specialists are also responsible for weeding the same areas of the collection on an ongoing basis.

Unfortunately, there is little published research comparing the effectiveness of the centralized versus the decentralized approach. It is clear that librarians "love" being responsible for a portion of the collection and making selections but too often "holes" within the collection develop as not enough people are available to cover the entire collection. For medium-size and smaller libraries, they're usually not enough professional librarians to utilize the decentralized approach.

- *Vendor approval plans.* Libraries can sign up for a vendor approval plan where the vendor assumes responsibility for making selections for one or more areas within the library's collection. While academic libraries usually use this approach, some public libraries have also found this approach to be helpful. The library completes a profile indicating what they would normally choose if they were making the selection decisions. The vendor uses this profile, along with a budget ceiling, to make selections, which are then purchased and forwarded to the library.

- *A combination.* Some libraries use a combination of the above methods to make selection decisions. Libraries need to consider the alternatives and the needs of their communities to decide what will be best for them.

Evidence-Based Selection

For the majority of public libraries, decisions about what to add to a collection are made on a title-by-title basis. Librarians making selection decisions rely on reviews in library journals, catalogs provided by publishers, and library vendors. This historical approach is never-the-less a very expensive process that libraries may wish to reexamine.

Some libraries are starting to experiment with patron-driven acquisitions (PDA), increasingly called demand-driven acquisitions (DDA), in order to deliver just-in-time materials of interest to the customer. The idea with DDA is that the customer requests an item and the library is able to quickly provide access to the desired item. Bibliographic information is loaded into the library's catalog, or a link is provided to a vendor's catalog, so that the customer may "discover" the availability of specific content of interest. If a customer wants to checkout a book, then an order is placed. For eBooks, the order is filled immediately; for print or other physical materials, there is a delay until the library receives the item. A majority of DDA efforts to date have been to provide access to eBooks (Swords 2011). Interestingly, publishers provide their metadata for free to *Bowker*, which proceeds to repackage it and sell it to retailers, wholesalers, and libraries. It would be interesting if publishers were to make their metadata more visible (discoverable via Internet search engine crawling spiders) as a free resource. This would improve the discovery of an eBook or pBook (or other materials such as audio books, DVDs, and so forth) by the individual using search engines.

Several variables will likely influence the degree to which demand-driven acquisitions may play a role in a library's efforts to provide the materials desired by their customers. These variables include:

- *Format*—some suppliers will only provide access to eBooks while others provide access to pBooks and other materials.

- *Unconventional sources*—purchasing an item from Amazon, Half .com, and other book suppliers may significantly reduce the cost of acquisitions.

- *Vendors*—as well as publishers may impose their own constraints on demand-driven acquisitions.

- *Multiple sources*—the availability of an item from multiple sources (with different prices and time to delivery) makes the situation a bit more complicated.

- *Short-term rentals*—rather than purchasing the desired item, the library may acquire the right to rent (and loan) an item for a short period of time.

- *Usage rights*—Some titles may be restricted to a single user at a time while others may support multiple simultaneous users.

Demand-driven acquisitions matches acquisition to immediate demand and allows the library to pay at the point of need, pay for amount of need, offer short-term loans, as well as purchase on demand options. The library can consider purchase rather than borrowing an item using interlibrary loan depending on the price, publisher, subject matter, and publication date. Some older items may be available from an Internet supplier for very low prices. Some libraries have achieved significant savings using demand-driven acquisitions as one component in their overall acquisitions efforts. For many libraries, the goal of demand-driven acquisitions are threefold: to reduce costs, to align the library's collection more closely with current users' immediate needs, and to present a much broader array of titles to patrons.

Summary of Findings

A library should periodically review its written collection development plan to ensure that it stays relevant given the rapid changes that are occurring in the environment surrounding the library. Library customers are changing the mix of materials that they would like to borrow/use from the library as other commercial and non-commercial options make their lives easier and more convenient. Involving the library customers in identifying what to purchase as well as considering establishing relationships with non-traditional vendors may make the library's collections more relevant and of value to the members of the community.

Take Action

A library can take a number of actions to ensure that its physical collections will have value (and thus used) by the community. Among these actions are:

- If it has been more than two years since your library management team has updated the library's collection development policy, do so now.

- Review and consider changes to the library's checkout loan periods (two weeks, three weeks, one week for popular materials, and so forth) so that the turnover rate for each item can be improved.

- Review and consider changes to the library's fine rates for overdue items. In addition, consider shortening the periods between overdue notices so that customers with overdue materials are turned over to a collection agency sooner (which will mean more materials will be returned to the library).

- Involve the library customer in identifying items that the library should add to its collections.

- Consider the use of approval plans to get new materials to the library quicker.

- Consider the use of one or more non-traditional sources for acquiring new materials in a cost-effective manner such as using Amazon .com, Half.com, or other online vendors.

7

Evaluating the Collection

If it ain't broke, break it, then fix it. Otherwise you may be destined to address tomorrow's problems with yesterday's solutions.

—Clark Crouch

Beware the Holy Grail! To gauge the impact of a service you need to know what change it is making, not what you hope it might do—evidence not aspirations.

—Sharon Markless

Creating and maintaining proactive collections takes the time and attention of many library staff members. A part of the time should be spent in carefully "listening" to the library's customers by carefully examining the actual use of the collections. The evaluation of a library's physical and digital collections will pay real dividends, as the library will be able to demonstrate:

- Transparency—proving that the materials purchased have been used and are of value to the community

- Accountability—proving that the funds provided by been carefully spent

- Responsiveness—providing materials that are desired and of real value to the customer

- Balance—acknowledging the tradeoffs of the costs of purchasing materials given economic constraints

The benefit to the library that employs these suggested methods is that they will be able to document for their funding stakeholders that the library is providing real value to its community.

109

While there are a variety of methods that may be employed to assist in evaluating a library's collection, it is possible to group these methods into two broad perspectives:

- *A library-centric view*—the focus is on analyzing collection size, quality, coverage by type of material, diversity of views

- *A customer-centric perspective*—the emphasis is on the amount of collection use and other measures of use of materials and who is using the materials.

The approach recommended here suggests that the proactive public library should implement a marketing-based evaluation approach that identifies:

- What's hot—what is heavily used

- What's not (hot)—what is lightly used or not used as all

- What's not (hot), but should be, in the collection

- What's inhibiting use of the collection

When conducting any evaluation, the quality of the effort is more important than spending significant amounts of time. Every library has an automated library system that will prepare a series of standard reports. In addition, almost all automated systems provide a tool that allows the librarian to prepare one or more ad hoc reports. The important thing is to identify a small set of reports and then prepare these reports on a regular and consistent basis. Tracking a small set of data, such as turnover rate by type of material, allows the library to identify any significant trends.

Caveat

The assumption about a marketing-based proactive library collection is that its collection closely matches the needs and interests of the community and thus the collection will receive heavier use. But use of the collection is also influenced by how the collection is stored and made accessible to the customer—traditional library shelving versus merchandising the library's collection. Further, most libraries do not track use of the collection within the library itself (e.g., when a book is taken from the shelf but not checked out). For some libraries, this in-house use can be fairly high and should actually be tracked and recorded for further analysis. Also, research has shown that past use is an accurate indicator of future use (Slote 1997; see also chapters 8 and 9 in Matthews 2007).

One final caveat is that when multiple methods are employed to analyze the library's physical and digital collections, the resulting picture that emerges is clearer and provides more details (if they are wanted).

What's Hot and What's Not?

The proactive public library routinely identifies material formats, subject areas, and genres that receive constant, heavy use. The automated library system will produce a variety of reports that can assist in this effort. Libraries should adopt use of four approaches that have proved to be fruitful over time. These approaches, from the general to the specific, include:

- Examining the total use by material type, genre, and subject categories
- Determining the relative use by range of classification number
- Examining the total usage of individual titles
- Examining the hold queues
- Examining the customer requests for items to be added to the collection.

Examining Totals by Class

Historically, almost every public library has kept statistics on the number of times items have been borrowed by:

- Material types (books, DVDs, CDs, picture books, e-books, magazines)
- Genres (westerns, science fiction, mysteries, romance, and so forth)
- Subjects (broad or narrow groupings within the Dewey Decimal Classification System such as the 100s, 300s, 500s, or breaking up the broad groups into smaller categories such as 310, 320, 330, and so forth)
- User groups (seniors, adults, young adults, children, and so forth)

The uses of such statistics help librarians guide their decisions of what materials to add to their collections, guide decisions about what to include in deposit collections and the bookmobile. Many libraries combine this usage data with the number of shelves occupied, volume count, and budget allocation to help guide their collection development decisions. Placing all of this data into a spreadsheet overcomes the time consuming and tedious task that this used to be for the acquisition staff members.

One of the principle benefits obtained from tracking the usage data of a class over time (three to five years) is that you can determine whether use is

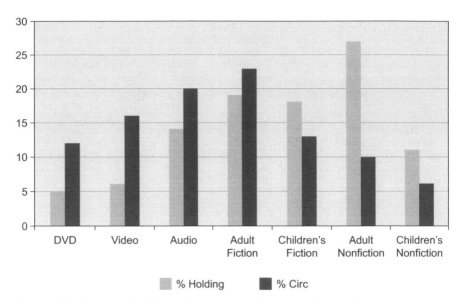

Figure 7.1. Percent Holdings Compared to Percent Circulation

increasing, decreasing, or remaining constant. The total circulation for each class is gathered and placed in a spreadsheet for each of the last three to five years. This data can be shown as a chart (see Figure 7.1) and the selection decisions can be adjusted based on what the data reveals. For example, it might be appropriate to increase spending in one area and decrease it in another.

Calculating the holdings turnover rate (the total annual circulation per class divided by the total number of items in the class) is another helpful measure to determine areas of the collection that are well used and those classes that received little use.

Douglas Galbi (2008) has analyzed more than a century of public library circulation data and found that on average library users borrowed about 15 books per user per year. However, since the early 1980s, about 25 percent of total circulation shifted from books to audiovisual materials. To date, no study has examined the amount of eBook borrowing in a public library.

As an interesting aside, an analysis by Ujiie and Krashen (2006) found that prize-winning children's books (Newbery and Caldecott awards) are sparsely represented on best seller lists, are not likely to be found in public library collections, and that use of the prize-winning books is less than books on the best seller lists. Whether this extends to adult reading material is an interesting question; but one might conclude from this evidence that collecting award-winning titles will not ensure filling your community's needs—at least in terms of children's literature.

Relative Use by Each Class

The annual circulation data by class can also be compared to the holdings within each class. Comparing percent circulation by class with percent holdings by class can reveal areas in which the library has greater holdings and less demand; and conversely identify areas where demand exceeds the percent holdings. This is illustrated in Figure 7.2. If the collection is closely matched to the interests and needs of a library's customers, we can logically expect that actual use will be proportional to the size of the class, however that class is defined.

A library should identify about 50 to 60 groups of classes of materials and routinely prepare a report that provides an analysis of relative use by each class. In addition, the subjects covered within a class should also be considered as a narrow topic within a class may provide disproportionate use. Consider a class composed of all items in the Dewey 650–659 range and that percent circulation is the same as percent holdings. However, books and other materials about résumés (650.14) may account for a disproportionate share of the circulation within the class.

Collection (Dewey range)	% of Items	% of Total Collection	Circulation	% of Total Circulation	% of Relative Use
001	3,384	1.42	5,519	2.14	150.70
010	1,219	.51	68	.03	5.88
020	1,509	.64	308	.12	18.75
030–099	1,611	.67	1,248	.48	71.64
100–199	6,451	2.71	4,719	1.83	67.53
200–299	8,714	3.66	5,413	2.10	57.38
300	4,573	1.92	6,891	2.67	139.06
310	2,369	.99	2,542	.99	100.00
320	3,216	1.35	1,876	.73	54.07
330	1,782	.75	1,407	.55	73.33
340	1,921	.81	2,984	1.16	143.21
350	2,799	1.17	4,621	1.79	152.99

Figure 7.2. Percent Holdings and Percent Circulation Report

Relative use figures can be calculated for format, genres, subject areas, reading levels, and so forth to assist in identifying collection strengths and weaknesses. Some public libraries have found that uncataloged paperback books account for a disproportionate amount of use; and thus these libraries have added more paperback books to their collections.

Rather than simply eyeballing the numbers in order to determine areas of overuse and underuse, Mills (1982) suggested that the library multiply the relative use factor (the percentage of use divided by the percentage of holdings) by 100 to create the percentage of expected use (PEU). This can be quickly accomplished when using a spreadsheet. Each class is then placed in rank order, from high to low. Once the standard deviation has been calculated, those classes with PEUs that is more than one standard deviation above or below the mean can be labeled as overused or underused.

Remember that many reasons may account for the under-use of a class of materials. Some of these reasons might include outdated materials, materials that are too technical or too specialized, or that the interests and needs of the community of users have changed.

Individual Item Usage

The library can also identify the usage for each individual title. Annually the library should prepare reports that show usage by title/item so that it can determine whether some of these items should be discarded (weeded). Stanley Slote (1997) identified the reality that every library has two collections: that part of the collection that is used and the collection that is not used. Each of these collections has similar characteristics in terms of their physical appearance, age of the item, subject matter, and so forth. Slote refers to these two collections as the *core collection* and the *noncore collection*.

Rick Lugg and Ruth Fischer (2009) suggest a two-part weeding rule—no item in the core collection should be considered for weeding while all items in the noncore collections should be weeded. If such a use-only weeding rule was followed, it would have no impact whatsoever on customer service and satisfaction. The real benefit of a use-only weeding rule is it would free up some space that the library could decide to use in other ways. In addition, if old non-used materials are retained, it frustrates customers as they attempt to locate a desired item among many other resources.

> *Favorite Definition of the Catalog*
> *A place where items get lost in alphabetical order.*

> *Favorite Definition of a Library Collection*
> *A place when items get lost in call number order.*

Before analyzing your collection, be sure to determine what constitutes little or no use. Comparing the item's turnover rate to the average turnover rate within the class should be a helpful indicator. For example, if the average turnover rate within a range of call numbers is ten, and a specific item's call number turnover is two (two uses per year), then this item becomes a candidate for weeding.

All of the above discussion considers only the use of circulation data for analysis. Research has shown (see chapter eight in Matthews 2007) that the amount of in-library use of the library's physical collection can range considerably (from 0.1:1—in-library use to patron borrowing—to more than 10:1). Some libraries routinely capture in-library usage data using their library's integrated library system by scanning each item that has been used in the library before it is returned to the shelf. The librarian is thus able to get a more accurate picture of the total use of the collection by class and by individual item.

Identifying Gaps

No library is able to meet 100 percent of what is desired by its customers. Thus, identifying what is not currently in the collection but could be added will help meet the needs of more customers. After all, an item sought by one customer is likely to be of interest to others in the community.

Librarians responsible for the collection can collect information about what should be added using several different methods:

- Analyzing interlibrary loan records
- Analyzing unanswered reference questions
- Asking customers to suggest items to add to the collection.
- Analyzing the use of the online catalog
- Using crowdsourcing or online surveys to "vote" for titles being considered
- Using a customer satisfaction survey to obtain timely feedback about how well the library is doing

Analyzing Interlibrary Loan Activity

When an interlibrary loan (ILL) request is received, many libraries automatically consider purchasing the item (especially if the item is less than two years old). Many studies show that interlibrary loan requests are for current, in print items, and that materials purchased as the result of an interlibrary loan request generally circulate better than other items in their class. Given the availability of older materials available for purchase on the Internet from many different sources (the long-tail effect), public libraries should also consider purchasing older materials rather than borrowing from another library. The costs of an interlibrary loan are significant (for both the borrowing and loaning libraries) and the customer must often wait for two to three weeks to receive a requested item. Purchasing an item may well be cheaper and quicker to fulfill a customer's request (ordering an item online, the library can receive it in two to three days and have it in the hands of the customer in another two to three days). In fact, some libraries already purchase ILL requests rather than borrowing the item from another library. Aside from getting the item in the hands of the customer faster, one study by Tyler et al. (2011) found that the turnover rate for ILL purchased materials was the highest when compared to firm orders, approval plans, lost books, and donor bequests.

At a minimum, a library should analyze ILL requests on a quarterly basis and examine the requests by format, genre, subject matter, and author. One popular report involves comparing percent holdings (by Dewey range) with percent ILL requests (by Dewey range). A library should consider bolstering its purchases in an area when the difference between the two percentages is greater than 10 percent (Ochola 2002).

Answering Unanswered Reference Questions

Many libraries record the subject matter of all reference questions that cannot be answered. This data can be used to improve the collection at little cost of staff time and improve customer satisfaction with the library.

Asking Customers to Suggest New Purchases

Asking your customers to suggest titles to add to the library's collection makes sense from so many different perspectives. Aside from providing a suggestion form (paper and online), a library should encourage staff to ask each customer whether they found what they were looking for (when the customer is leaving the library or at the circulation desk if the customer interacts with staff). Staff can then record, using a variety of tools, items that people were looking for but did not find.

Analyzing the Use of the Online Catalog

The library can periodically run a report of its automated library system that identifies the online catalog search requests that failed. Of particular interest would be the failed title searches, but failed author and subject searches should also be reviewed. The report from most automated library systems can be produced in alphabetical order and will assist in identifying new works that the library should consider adding to its collection.

Using Crowdsourcing to "Vote" for Titles Being Considered

There is considerable evidence that a group of people are able to make better decisions than one single individual or a small group of staff members (Sloan 2011; Howe 2008; and Surowiecki 2005). Some libraries have placed bibliographic records (either in a separate file or in the library's online catalog) and asked customers to vote on items they would like to see the library add to the collection. Given the shrinking acquisition's budgets in recent years, getting customers involved seems a better way to ensure that materials that are purchased are of real interest and will be used.

Customer Satisfaction Survey

A library can subscribe to a service such as Counting Opinions LibSAT® so that the library receives feedback on an ongoing basis as to how well it is doing. The real value of the survey, in addition to tracking trends over time, is that about 40 percent of the respondents will provide comments to open-ended questions about the library's collections, its services, staff, facilities, and so forth. These comments, often quite long and insightful, can be periodically reviewed to learn how well the library is doing.

Collection Analysis Tools

A library can choose to use a commercial collection analysis tool (on a one shot basis or on a continuing ongoing basis) to help improve the use of its collections. Two major options are available:

- OCLC's WorldCat Collection Analysis tool
- Baker & Taylor's *CollectionHQ* tool

The OCLC WorldCat Collection Analysis tool compares one library's collection against the holdings in the entire WorldCat database and with selected other OCLC member libraries. Comparing the collection of one library with other peer libraries is a time-honored tradition that allows a library to identify its relative strengths and weaknesses so that it can improve its collection. Some libraries have successfully used such an analysis to garner additional funding to build or strengthen its collection (Monroe-Gulick and Currie 2012).

Baker & Taylor's *collectionHQ* tool, originally developed in England, extracts data from a library's integrated library system (ILS) on a regular basis, and then provides access to the data analysis using a suite of Web-based modules to build a plan to build and deploy a library's physical collections (Kelley 2012). *CollectionHQ* clearly identifies what materials a library should buy and in what quantities to meet customer demand. The system comes with a wide range of reports that are immediately available online in a user-friendly format. This obviates the need to turn to the integrated library system and generate a standard report or attempt to create a custom report (which in many systems is still a difficult task). Many of the larger U.S. and Canadian public libraries have signed up for the service. Costs range from $10,000 to $40,000 per year, based on the size of the library. Customers report that items fair quickly move to branches where they are more likely to appeal to the customers visiting a particular branch. Implicit within the *collectionHQ* approach is that collections must float to better meet customer demand.[1] One encouraging aspect is that any library can recreate the same benefits using the tools suggested in this book without signing up for the annual subscription costs of *collectionHQ*.

Availability Analysis

An availability study examines the reasons customers are unable to find the items they are looking for when they visit the library. An availability study has also been called a "shelf availability study," a "frustration study," or "failure study." Such studies have been conducted chiefly at academic libraries. The reasons an item might not be available range from being it checked out, missing, or misplaced on the shelf, to the customer searching incorrectly or the item not being owned by the library. In general, these studies reveal that a library customer only has about a 60 percent chance of getting the desired item (Nisonger 2007).

Other methods include:

- Obtaining a sample from the shelf list
- Using citations selected by experts in a subject field, and
- Using indexes, abstracts, or general bibliographies

A sample drawn from the shelf list of a library is unlikely to be a good one for use in studies of item availability because it over-represents items that have low or very low levels of demand. Paul Kantor (1981) suggested an approach that overcomes this bias.

Generally, more useful information can be obtained by using the customer as the source of the desired titles. This approach can be characterized as a customer-centric method. Involving the customers is a method that asks them to

---

We need your help!

Today we are studying availability of library materials. Please use this form to report which items you are looking for in the library. We want to know whether or not you were able to find these items on the shelf. This study will help us analyze the reasons that materials are not always readily available.

If you want the library to notify you if and when we find items that you cannot find today, please ask at the Circulation Desk as usual. We need this completed form in any case.

Thanks for your cooperation!

Author and Title	Call Number	Did Not Find Item (Check)	Found Item? (Check)

Please drop off this form on your way out.

Figure 7.3. Sample Material Availability Study Data Collection Form

record on a form what they are looking for and whether the desired items are found. The forms are distributed as the customer enters the library. Alternatively, a staff member could interview customers as they begin their search. The completed forms are then analyzed by staff to determine the cause of failure, if any. A sample data collection form is shown in Figure 7.3.

The availability study is examining the success of the library's collection when the customer is looking for a known item. This approach, which can be easily adapted for use in any type of library, has studied both monograph and serials collections. A similar analysis could be done concerning the library's electronic resources using an online survey (although this has yet to be done).

The sample sizes of the availability studies previously conducted range from slightly more than 200 to more than 2,300, with an average of about 800. The library management team will have more confidence in the results of an analysis with a larger sample size, but this needs to be balanced with the costs associated with the data collection effort.

Kantor (1984, 1976) developed a branching technique to illustrate the relationship between the various categories (see Figure 7.4). Available items were seen as flowing through a pipeline, some being sidetracked along branches for various reasons and thus contributing to the unavailability of a desired item. Those items emerging at the bottom of the pipe were available for use by the customer. Probabilities are calculated using the number of items that made it past the branch divided by the number of items that approached the branch.

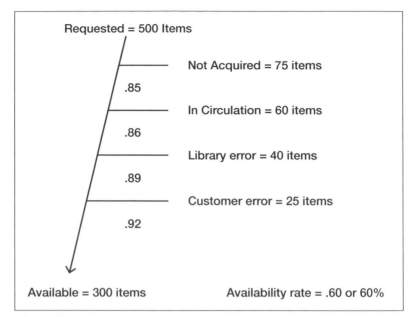

Requested = 500 Items

.85

Not Acquired = 75 items

.86

In Circulation = 60 items

.89

Library error = 40 items

.92

Customer error = 25 items

Available = 300 items   Availability rate = .60 or 60%

Figure 7.4. Kantor's Branching Diagram

Reasons an item might not be available include the following:

- **Collection Failure:** The library does not own the desired item or the desired item has been ordered and received but has not yet been processed (a processing backlog exists). The availability studies have shown that a collection failure occurs about 10 percent of the time. An analysis of customer requests to purchase titles for the collection as well as of interlibrary loan requests can assist in reducing customer frustrations.

- **In Circulation:** The desired item has been checked out to another customer or is on the hold shelf waiting to be checked out. This happens, on average, for about 15 to 20 percent of the items.

- **Library Error:** The item should be on the shelf but it is waiting to be shelved (yet to be sorted, on a sorting shelf or a book truck), is missing, is reported lost, or is shelved incorrectly. While there is some variation reported in the studies, library error averages about 13 percent.

- **Catalog Error:** The customer cannot find the item in the catalog. This occurs about 7 percent of the time. Among the factors that might be examined are the complexity of the user interface with the library's online catalog, the clarity of information (information overload) displaced as the result of a search, the number of mis-spellings in the catalog, and so forth.

- **Customer Error:** The customer brings an incorrect citation, wrote down the call number incorrectly (or relies on memory), does not understand how the Dewey Decimal System works (especially with long numbers), can't find a particular section in the library (where are the oversize books found anyway?), or can't locate the item on the shelf. Customer error averages about 10 percent.

The Kantor branching diagram approach has been used in a number of academic libraries (Palis 1981; Rinkel and McCandless 1983), a specialized academic library (Rashid 1990), a public library (Wood et al. 1990), and a study of the availability of periodicals (Murfin 1980). Haseeb Rashid suggested that a broader perspective that captured information about more categories of failure or disappointment would assist a library management team in understanding how they could make improvements. Rashid (1990) proposed 13 categories that should be tracked:

- Quality of information brought to the library by the patron
- Whether the title is owned by the library
- If the item is now owned by the library, whether the item meets the collection development policies of the library
- Whether the call number is recorded correctly
- Whether the item is located in a special collection/location identified in the library catalog
- Whether the item is located in a special collection/location *not* identified in the library catalog
- Whether the item has been properly shelved but not located by the patron
- Whether it has been mis-shelved
- Whether the item is in use in the library
- Whether it has been checked out
- Whether the item is in a pre-shelving area
- Whether it is missing, reported lost, or stolen
- Other factors

Anne Ciliberti (1987) expanded on the Kantor branching diagram by slightly revising the model for known-item searching and developed a parallel model for subject searching. She and her colleagues further elaborated the model by identifying the hurdles encountered in journal title searches (Ciliberti et al. 1998). This latter study revealed a number of problems that customers encountered that were unsuspected by library staff, including the need for better inventory control, better signage, and removing abbreviations from the catalog.

Another study, by Eugene Mitchell et al. (1994), successfully applied the Kantor branching diagram to subject searches and found the approach to be helpful in identifying needed improvements for the library's procedures. Three primary factors affect availability of a particular item: the item's popularity (best-seller list, recommendations, and so forth), the number of copies available for loan, and the length of the loan period (Buckland 1975).

It is also important to recognize that the 80/20 rule applies to most public library collections. That is, 20 percent of the most circulated items account for 80 percent (or more) of the total circulation (Britten 1990). Another study found that high intensity borrowers do exist, borrow weekly or more frequently, persist in their borrowing over years of time, and probably account for an overwhelming percentage of a public library's total circulation. These high intensity borrowers also borrow materials for others in their family—sometimes-called surrogate borrowing (Clark 1998).

When a proactive public library plans to conduct an availability study, several suggestions will make the results more revealing:

- Make sure that the study separates the results for each facility as availability rates will likely vary by location

- An adequate sample size at each location of about five hundred requests will help ensure the reliability of the data

- Availability rates are likely to vary by format of the material

- A library can improve the number of people who participate by informing customers to the study and its value to them and how the library will use the results to improve the library's collections.

Floating Collections

Almost without exception, every public library with one or more branches maintains a "home" library location for every item in its collection. When an item is returned to a library other than its "home" or owning library, the item is flagged and the item is transported or moved to its home location. As the number of branches increases, the number of items being moved can increase significantly, especially as the library provides the ability for customers to place requests (hold) for items regardless of their location. The costs associated with moving items around a library system can be significant in terms of the costs associated with the purchase and maintenance of one or more vehicles, bins to handle the materials, and associated staff costs.

Another important cost often overlooked is the amount of time an item is waiting to move to another location, the actual in-transit time, and the time waiting to be placed on a shelf once the materials have arrived at the new location. For some library systems, this time can range from three to four days per movement!

One interesting alternative to the "owning" library concept is to use "floating collections." That is the collection is allowed to float and items are retained at the location where they are returned rather than being shipped back to their "home" library. Libraries that have adopted floating collections have noted that their transportation costs are significantly reduced and that library customers get items of interest more quickly. The Jefferson County (CO) Public Library and the Araphoe (CO) Library District moved to the use of floating collections and discovered that:

- Materials availability increased significantly
- One system, one collection
- Collections with a limited number of items or audience typically do not float
- Most libraries phase-in the floating process one collection at a time (but there are exceptions)
- The need to weed extensively prior to starting the "floating" process
- The locations that receive the returned materials from the patrons become the de facto weeding branches
- Collections are being continuously refreshed
- Customers have a more consistent experience moving from branch to branch
- Reduces the costs of material handling
- Reduces the impact on the environment (fewer trips)
- Reduces ergonomic injuries, and
- Extends the materials budget (Cress et al. 2007; Schneider 2009; Bartlett 2012).

The Vancouver (British Columbia) Public Library established a number of goals when they first started to implement floating collections (Johal and Quigley 2012):

- Increase the availability of items on the shelf
- Reduce the amount of items in transit
- Reduce the workload of delivery staff and library assistants who must deal with delivery materials (both sending and receiving)
- Refresh the collections at all locations
- Let the collections move itself

Other libraries that have embraced floating collections with positive results include the Contra Costa (CA) Library System (Franklin et al. 2005), the Hennepin County (MN) Library (Cherry et al. 2004), the Sarasota County (FL) Library System (Ginsky 2012), the Brown County (WI) Library (Cropper 2012), among many others. And the use of floating collections need not be restricted to a single library system as several Montana libraries joined together to implement a "seamless" system of floating collections (Bray and Langstaff 2007).

In a survey of 25 other North American public libraries that had implemented floating collections conducted by Johal and Quigley (2012), the most common challenges were:

- Lack of space on shelves
- Managing shortages and overflows
- Effective and consistent communication methods for distribution/redistribution
- Staff reluctance to weed
- Maintenance issues. Floating requires ongoing review (it will not take care of itself)
- Deciding what collections to float and what to exclude
- The need to encourage staff input, and
- The need to fine-tune the current practices.

The Edmonton (Alberta, Canada) Public Library has implemented a floating policy for all of its 1.6 million items over several years and has found that (Brown Canty et al. 2012):

- A marked reduction of materials in transit while experiencing a steady increase in circulation
- A 68 percent increase in customer holds
- Standardized and centralized acquisitions and processing
- More immediate delivery of new materials to customers

• Reduced damage to materials due to diminished materials handling formerly experienced in transit.

eResources

Libraries provide access to electronic content by listing the journal name or the name of the database on the library's Web site. No longer is the issue the need to balance print with serials and other audiovisual materials. The challenge facing any library today is to maintain a balance between print and eResources. Among the many factors involved in this balancing act are: customer needs, quality, relevance, value, depth and coverage, initial and ongoing costs, license versus purchase, and so forth.

The individual user who wants access to these electronic resources needs to be authenticated (have a library card or other valid identification) so that the terms of the licensing agreement with the vendor are followed. The value of eResources from the customer's perspective is the immediate (anytime, anywhere, any device) access to electronic content. Many librarians believe that rather than attempting to replace print materials (which is being done for reference materials), eResources actually complement existing collections.

Over the last ten years, the growth of the library's budget devoted to the licensing of electronic resources has steadily increased. A series of surveys indicated that most users of electronic resources, even after logging in to gain access to electronic resources using the library's Web site, are unaware of the costs and effort required to make these resources accessible. Thus, more and more of the library's services are becoming even more invisible.

For example, the OCLC *Perceptions* report (2005) surveyed 3,348 respondents from seven English-speaking countries. This report found that 84 percent of individuals started a search for information using an Internet search engine (slightly more than a third of people used Google). Only 1 percent used their academic or public library as a starting point! And respondents rated search engines higher than libraries in terms of quality and quantity of information.

An update of the OCLC Perceptions report (2010) found that more than two-thirds of those surveyed now used Google (and even more people use Google today). In 2010, 84 percent of people start looking for information using a search engine and not a single respondent reported starting with a library Web site. Use of library-provided eResources held steady at about 16 percent in 2005 and 2010.

Surprisingly only 16 percent of respondents had ever used an online database and only 30 percent had ever used a library Web site. These results are contrasted with the fact that 72 percent had used free search engines such as Google. A Pew Internet & American Life Project report (2012) noted, 55 percent of users completely agree that Google supplies worthwhile information while only 31 percent say the same for library databases. Furthermore, library-supplied information is not trusted any more than free Internet-based information. Clearly, people are speaking with a very loud voice that convenience trumps everything during the information search process.

One of the continuing challenges facing all libraries is that the library "brand" can be captured in one word—books! Yet most libraries devote little or none of their budget to marketing in an effort to suggest that the library is more than books. Most information consumers are not aware of, and do not use, the library's electronic information resources. And college students, who are intensive users of the library, indicate that their library's collections (physical and electronic) do not meet their information needs. Most students use an information-seeking and research strategy driven by efficiency and predictability for managing and controlling all of the information resources available to them on college campuses (Head and Eisenberg 2010).

Obviously most every public library customer wants to gain access to electronic information—it's just that the library might not be the place that they start or ever visit. Yet, the library really has no option but to provide some access to electronic resources to their users. This reality about the need to provide access to electronic resources has a number of implications.

First, more and more of a library's budget is being devoted to providing these electronic resources. The vendors of these electronic resources, be they a publisher or an aggregator, are only providing a license to gain access and not purchase the electronic journals or database themselves. Thus, a library is faced with the grim reality that more and more of their budget is constrained by the fixed costs of providing access to these electronic resources year and year. And the vendors, of course, typically raise their subscription prices each and every year— even in the harsh financial times facing public libraries.

Second, the library is unable to add access to single electronic journals as most journal and magazine publishers either provide access to all of the journals that they publish or have signed agreements with an aggregator to provide access to their journal(s). Thus, when an additional electronic resource is added to what the library already provides, the additional resource typically provides access to a number of electronic resources or journals rather than a single journal or magazine. At a higher cost, regardless whether the library needs these other journals.

Third, publishers and aggregators can restrict library and patron access more than ever by limiting access in their licensing agreements. This has introduced a fundamental change between the library and how some information is made accessible to the library's customers. Rather than controlling the resource (as is the case when an item is purchased), the library is now licensing content that is owned (and controlled) by a third party. Publishers and third party aggregators enjoy a monopoly position when dealing with the library. One positive way to counteract the power of publishers and aggregators is to form or join a cooperative in order to leverage the power of multiple libraries gaining access to the content (and being able to negotiate reduce prices for each of the participating libraries).

Fourth, the selection of electronic resources provided by the library determines what market segments of the local community use these electronic resources (if a customer is interested in business-related resources and the library does not license an appropriate resource, then the customer is out of luck). Unlike the physical library where the library is able to provide a collection of physical materials that best meets the needs of the local community, the choice of electronic resources will determine who actually uses the electronic resources provided by the public library. For example, if electronic genealogical resources are not provided then those interested in documenting their family trees will need to look elsewhere for these resources. In general, libraries are able to respond fairly quickly to a purchase request for a specific item but have greater difficulty in responding to request to gain access to specific electronic journals or databases.

The other real challenge facing libraries is the need to measure the usage level of each electronic resource (vendors and publishers are typically required to provide monthly usage statistics for each subscription). The cruel reality was that each of the vendor's reports measured things in different ways and called things by different names. This led to an initiative called COUNTER (Counting Online Usage of NeTworked Electronic Resources) in which a committee of vendors and librarians developed a set of specifications and practices that brought consistency to the vendor provided monthly statistics. Yet, the process of gathering and analyzing COUNTER-compliant statistics remains difficult. Another initiative, called SUSHI (Standards Usage Statistics Harvesting Initiative), provides a standardized process by which COUNTER statistics can be downloaded into the library's electronic resource management system. Despite the progress made by vendors and libraries, the COUNTER reports still do not provide a cost per use report and the library is unable to download statistics that conform to their fiscal year (Welker 2012).

Many libraries combine the usage statistics with cost information to calculate a cost per usage (downloads for example) to provide an indication as to the value of each electronic resource. And while cost per download is an important metric, it is also important to use caution when attempting to calculate cost per download figures (Bucknell 2012).

Summary of Findings

In this chapter a series of tools that any library can easily use to evaluate their library's collections were presented and discussed. A collection that is regularly weeded and has new materials added on a regular basis is likely to be used more than a collection that is not. However, the library must delve deeper by looking at what segments of the collection are used and identify those areas that are receiving little or no use. The goal is to shape a collection over time that is responsive to the needs of the total community as well as to each market segment that have been identified by the library that it will be serving.

Take Action

Consider a variety of actions in order to evaluate its current collections, policies, and services so that improvements can be made. The goal is for a library to be more responsive to all of its customers. Among these actions are:

- Task a small team to prepare an availability analysis for your library in order to discover the underlying causes as to why library customers are unable to obtain a copy of a desired item when the author's name and/or title is known. If your library's available rate is below 60 percent, this should be a cause for concern and concerted action to improve your library's availability rate.

- Using the library's integrated library system (ILS), prepare a report of what materials have the highest demand (what's hot).

- Using the library's integrated library system (ILS), prepare a report of what materials have little or no demand (what's not hot). This report can then be used to weed the collection.

- Consider the results of the two reports noted above and see if you can identify what type of materials should, in your opinion, be receiving more attention and use. Should the library relocate one or more locations so that they are noted more quickly when someone enters the library? Should signage be improved? Should resources be promoted on the library Web site or in the library newsletter?

- If your library has branch locations, consider implementing a floating collection policy for several types of materials. This will save the library transportation costs and improve the availability of desired materials in each location.

- Calculate the cost per use of electronic resources using COUNTER-compliant data from each vendor. If the costs are high, consider eliminating a subscription to the resource and obtain the needed resources in a more cost-effective manner.

Note

1. For more information about *collectionHQ*, visit http://www.collectionhq.com/

Providing Access

*Borrowing the best of bookstore models makes librar-
ies more usable.*
It's not about Dewey.

—Francine Fialkoff

*Seventy million books in America's libraries, but the
one you want to read is always out.*

—Tom Masson

Public libraries were created around a central idea: to make available
shared (principally print-based) resources that can be used by all members of
the community in order to stimulate imagination and inquiry, and nurture the
development of culture and commerce. Libraries offer a range of products and
services that are open to all and, it is hoped, will benefit those who choose to
use the physical (and/or virtual) library. It is the combination of community and
choice, provided by publicly supported funding for private benefit, which makes
the concept of the public library so special.

This chapter explores the various options that are available to provide
physical access to library collections and services. Chapter 7 explored the implications for providing access to electronic resources using the library's Web site
and other tools such as the library's catalog.

Types of Facilities

One of the clear challenges facing a library in any community is where
to locate a library and, if and when the size of the community grows, where
to place additional library facilities. There have been a plethora of studies that
have examined the importance of distance as a factor in determining use of a
library. The principal conclusion of these studies is that the impact of distance is

not a simple and constant factor but rather that distance is influenced by socio-economic status of the community, on the age of the residents, and on the characteristics of the library itself and any barriers to access that naturally occur, e.g., a river, a freeway, and so forth. The use of a library by children is clearly influenced by distance (that is, the closer a child lives to a library the more likely they are to use it) whereas an adult is willing to travel farther (especially if the library is "appealing" for some reason).

For many people, safety and "ease of use" are really what drives the decision to visit a particular organization. Saving time of the customer should be one of the driving forces behind any library's decision to reframe what the library means to the community.

In medium and large size communities, the assumption is often made that a central or main library building is needed. This ignores two very important and fundamental questions that should be asked. First, is a central library really needed? The answer depends upon the needs of the community being served. In addition, it is important to recognize that the library does not exist in a vacuum. Some communities are surrounded by good public libraries that are located in other jurisdictions as well as one or more large academic institutions. For example, citizens living in the Seattle area live in a "library rich environment" with a significant number of branch facilities (in the city of Seattle as well as the surrounding King County) in addition to the large downtown public library and academic libraries to choose from. Also, community members can generally go online to access the collections of any library, place a reserve on the item they want, and arrange to have it picked up in a location most convenient to them. So the need for a central library must be carefully considered. Second, if a central library is needed, then what are the roles and responsibilities of the main library compared to the role of the branches?

One obvious question that arises about the need to build one or more branch libraries is "What kind of branch library should be built?" There are two general options:

- A "full service" branch

- A specialized branch

A full service branch library offers almost all of the services found in a main library except that the building, collections, and staff levels are smaller. A specialized branch focuses on meeting the needs of a niche market segment and exclude all non-relevant library services. Each of these options is discussed in greater detail below.

Full-service Branch Libraries

Branch libraries were originally viewed as a distributing agency and advertising for the main library. This began to change in the 1940s starting with a landmark study of the Chicago Public Library by Carleton Joeckel and Leon Carnovsky (1940), who were faculty members of the Graduate Library School at the University of Chicago, when they suggested that the library system expand the number of and the variety of services offered in a branch library. The authors found that a vast majority of the customers relied solely on the resources and services of the neighborhood branch library and few used the branch as a stepping-stone to the main library.

Lowell Martin, one of the library profession's pre-eminent public library planning and building consultants, completed his master's thesis in 1940. Martin's thesis was the foundation upon which he developed a series of ideas and recommendations that were included in a series of major planning studies done for many large library systems throughout the United States over the course of the next forty years. The continuing themes that are reflected in these planning reports include:

- The need for three levels of library facilities—smaller neighborhood branches, larger regional libraries, and a main or central library. The branch library was to serve a local clientele whose reading demands were limited in scope. Regional libraries provide access to a broader range of materials and services. And the central library was to house the largest collection and act as a community "research" library.

- The fact that branch libraries have a different mission than the main library and should be treated as a discrete unit with very specific collections, services, and facilities that were designed to meet the needs of the local community. As such, branch library collections should focus on high demand materials and not attempt to provide a "well rounded" collection.

- The belief that all library facilities should be providing access to audiovisual materials.

- The idea that books and other materials in branch libraries should be organized in an "interest arrangement" rather than by one of the more traditional classification schemes (Dewey or Library of Congress call numbers). The intent of the subject interest grouping of materials is to provide good books (recent) and then "draw the visitor's attention to them." This sounds very similar to the topic of merchandising of a library's collection! Martin suggested using a series of broad subject grouping of nonfiction books with classification numbers disregarded. Fiction materials could also be organized by categories for readers seeking diversion and recreation.

Yet, despite these studies most library systems have created branch library facilities that provide much of what can be found in a main library (given building space constraints):

- A children's collection featuring numerous picture books
- An area to hold children story hours
- A popular adult fiction collection
- A nonfiction collection
- An audiovisual (media) collection
- A reference desk staffed by one or more reference librarians
- A print reference collection
- A number of computers that provide Internet access
- A meeting room
- The usual collection of tables and chairs
- A circulation desk

For a majority of public libraries, every branch library has been treated as all others (making adjustments for size). Thus, new materials are allocated on a formula basis to all branches in the name of equality without regard to the fact that some portions of the collection are more heavily used than others in one branch compared to another branch. The needs and interests in a neighborhood surrounding a branch are different but is typically not recognized when planning library collections and services. The goal for most libraries is to provide a "balanced" collection with some material on most subjects, waiting on the shelves for the possible user.

Thus, a very important part of planning for branch library facilities is to have a clear and explicit statement about the role of the branch library. Simply acknowledging financial realities suggests that most branch libraries should provide greater access to a collection of physical materials and services that are specifically targeted to meet the particular needs of the community in which it is located rather than attempting to provide a "balanced" collection.

A recent report prepared by the Urban Libraries Council (2005) reported on the efforts of the Chicago Public Library to foster branch libraries so that the library is at the center of the local community's life. A library can serve as an anchor for neighborhoods and communities. The libraries accomplished this by reaching out and building a bridge to the community by engaging with key individuals and partnering with other community organizations. The branch collections are reflective of the interests and languages spoken in the local community. Collaborating with other organizations has resulted in the development of innovative programs such as financial literacy classes, free children's passes to museums, among others. The key to such a strategy is to ensure that branch librarians and other staff members have outgoing personalities so that they really like engaging with members of the community.

An analysis of the branch libraries in New York City revealed that neighborhoods with a high percentage of populations of Asians and whites and low percentages of populations of Hispanics and blacks have higher public library use. And education (percent of adult population with a high school or better education is the second strongest predictor of public library use (Japzon and Gong 2005).

Christie Koontz (1997) suggested that the location of branch libraries is too important to leave to the simplicity of past siting and location criteria. She comes to these conclusions based on a review of the literature that demonstrates: 1) location is a major determent of use, 2) public libraries, through optimal location, should be accessible to the greatest number of users, and 3) retail site selection methods, including use of geographical-based mapping systems, would be of value when making a siting decision (Koontz 2007).

Differences in overall circulation levels by branch are related to the social and economic characteristics of the populations being served. Yet, despite socioeconomic differences in a community, the overall distribution in circulation across subject categories for all branches is relatively small (Ottensmann et al. 1995).

Given that the vast majority of branch libraries are all very similar in terms of collections and services provided then it is quite clear that most librarians, library building consultants, and architects have assumed that all new branch libraries should also be similar. However, it is possible to consider other options for a branch library.

> *Traditional Libraries reach traditional users.*
> *Nontraditional libraries reach everybody.*
> —Michelle Gorman in Kenny (2005)

Unique or narrowly-focused libraries

Another option for a branch library is to create a library that is narrowly focused and designed to meet the needs of a specific segment of the population. Hopefully you have gone through the process of identifying different market segments that the library has and has not been serving and will know what type of unique library would best fit in your community. Public libraries in North America, Asia, Europe, and South America have been designing and building unique libraries. A number of these narrowly focused libraries are discussed in greater detail in this chapter. These unique libraries have been described as a "niche library," a "boutique library," or a "lifestyle library."

The National Library Board in Singapore is responsible for the operation of all public libraries, community college libraries, government agency libraries, and one university library. Starting in the year 2000, the National Library Board has been transforming itself by reinventing libraries. The mission of the library is to expand the learning capacity of the nation. The service vision is to deliver services that are convenient, accessible, affordable, and useful. The transformation focused on four building blocks—content, services, people, and infrastructure.

The public libraries in Singapore used the transformation opportunity to prototype new facilities and services rather than relying on "plain vanilla" libraries. These test beds allowed staff to improve on the prototypes and the successful ideas and concepts were then incorporated into new buildings and rolled out to existing branches.

The library has 23 library facilities. The use of these facilities in Singapore has jumped substantially from 2000 to 2006: annual visits from 5.7 million to 38 million; circulation from 10 million to 29 million; inquiries from 50,000 to 2.8 million. At the same time the age of the collections have decreased from 11.5 years to less than 5 years! And by 2010, circulation has increased to more than 33 million items and the number of cardholders is now more than 2 million.

Like many library systems in the states, Singapore has built three very large regional libraries—about 120,000 square feet in size and that contain a collection of some 500,000 items. Each regional library has four floors, each of which is targeted to a different market segment—reference, children, young adult (with large study areas), and adult. Circulation in each of these libraries runs more than two million items annually.

A number of libraries have experimented with providing different types of facilities as well as new ways of delivering library services.[1] Among these are three examples from Singapore:

- Community children's libraries that are specifically designed for children that range in age from 4 to 10 years old. Everything is designed for these small "customers" including the furniture, the collection and services.

- Adult Community Library serves the adults of a local community and, as such, provides popular fiction, nonfiction, and audiovisual materials.

- Shopping mall libraries, located in the key regional shopping malls, are focused on the young adult segment of the population. These libraries have collections that are primarily audiovisual in nature along with a small collection of popular magazines (Chia 2001).

- Cerritos (CA) has created an "Experience Library" in a large facility that offers a rich experience for any visitor including a 15,000-gallon saltwater aquarium at the entrance to the unique multimedia learning centers, to "themed" spaces to define its different collections. "InfoStations" extend customer service to points throughout the building. Electronic resources include some 200-computer workstations, 1,200 laptop ports, wireless access, and a state-of-the-art computer lab. Multimedia learning centers integrate print materials with Web resources and computer graphics. This is a library that simply hums with excitement and energy.

- Tower Hamlets, located in London's East End, is characterized by high unemployment, low education levels, poor occupational skills, and a diverse population (more than 50 languages are spoken). Use of the public libraries in this area had fallen quite dramatically. Working closely with the community the library reached a surprising conclusion. Reinvent the library! Thus a partnership with the borough's Office of Lifelong Learning Services was formed to combine adult and recreational education with traditional library functions. Thus was born the concept of a new brand—The Idea Store! The new modern facilities are flexible in design and permit the integration of educational, community, and library services. A café is provided to encourage people to relax, read, and chat.

- The DOK, located in the city of Delft, in the Netherlands, is a media center that combines three collections: Music and film, literature, and art. These three collections together with the expertise of the staff form the foundation for the flow of creativity and energy of the individuals who visit the DOK. The attraction of the DOK is emphasized by the fact that more than 500,000 visit the library each year and that they must purchase an annual membership card.

Recognizing that the world is changing rapidly and that the Internet is making walls and boundaries disappear, the focus of the DOK is to keep, make, and share stories—regardless of the medium (Boekesteijn 2008).

- DOK opened its new building in 2007, which provides a colorful and aesthetically-pleasing library—in short, **a destination**. Graphics for banners are colorful and attractive and natural language names are used to identify collections rather than a call number range. Comfortable furniture is provided and the goal is to encourage each visitor to have fun! Flexibility in this new building is a central design element—for example, shelving is mounted on casters so that it can be moved to create space for activities.

- ImaginOn is a joint venture of the Public Library of Charlotte & Mecklenburg County and the Children's Theatre of Charlotte that built a combined children's library and theater. The mission of ImaginOn is to "bring stories to life through extraordinary experiences that challenge, inspire and excite young minds"—in short, *a place to have fun!* ImaginOn is housed in a 102,000 square-foot facility. Wayfinding within ImaginOn is intuitive as light, sight, and color are effectively used.

- The Queens (NY) Library created a bright and welcoming teen's library using leased space near its existing branch in Far Rockaway, New York. Chairs, tables, and partitions are on wheels to allow for rearrangement to accommodate various activities. The library is only open during after-school hours.

- The Aarhus Public Library in Denmark has developed a project they called The Transformation Lab that is designed to answer the question: "When everything is available online, why come to the library at all?"

- Most importantly the library encourages the active participation of the customer as a real partner and collaborator. The user involvement in possible prototypes is all about "co-creation."

Other Options

In addition to the library constructing facilities, the library has other alternatives for providing access to library materials. Among these options are: deposit collections, personal delivery, delivery by mail, a materials dispensing machine, bookmobiles, and print-on-demand services.

Deposit Collections

Some libraries will deposit a small collection of materials with a partnering organization. The partnering organization (a senior center, a community center) assumes responsibility for providing access to the collection and maintaining control of the collection (borrowing, returning, tracking overdue and missing items). In some cases the materials are displayed with a label that encourages people to "Read and Return" the item to the local public library. In many cases, each item in the deposit collection contains an invitation to visit the local library in order to find "more items like this."

The library periodically refreshes the deposit collection. Normally the deposit collection only includes high-interest fiction and nonfiction items.

The library usually tailors the small collection to the needs of the client group. Deposit collections have been established at:

- Doctors and dentist offices (children's books)
- Hospital waiting rooms
- Correctional facilities
- Preschool and day care centers
- Homeless and women's shelters
- Community centers
- Senior centers
- Commercial stores
- County courthouse (jury duty rooms)
- Subway and commuter train stations

Personal Delivery

Some public libraries provide a delivery service for people in their homes, offices, hospitals, and so forth (the delivery service may be restricted to those that are house-bound or no restrictions may be enforced). The library maintains a personal profile for each recipient that indicates their reading/listening interests and what they have previously borrowed. Each recipient is visited on a scheduled periodic basis and materials are exchanged. Should the library provide a vehicle and a staff member to provide a personalized delivery service, it should be quite clear that the associated costs are fairly high.

Some libraries have recruited volunteers to provide a personalized delivery service. The volunteers need to be recruited, trained, and supervised by a library staff member.

Delivery by Mail

Another option for providing access is the delivery of library materials to the home of the customer. The materials are placed in a canvas pouch or box and a delivery service is used (U.S. Post Office, UPS, or a local delivery service). Materials can be ordered using the library's online catalog accessed via the library's Web site. In some cases, only paperback books, DVDs, and CDs will be delivered. The delivery of library materials by mail is particularly effective when serving large geographic areas with small rural populations or very large communities.

A more specialized delivery of materials is the Library of Congress's National Library Service for the Blind and Physically Handicapped. Recordings of books and magazines are sent to qualified individuals.

Some libraries have developed a paper-based catalog, which is distributed to each home in the library's service area. The catalog features new recently published materials and the catalog is typically distributed on a quarterly basis. Some libraries pick up the costs associated with returning materials while other libraries expect the patrons to pay for the return of materials.

Materials Dispensing Machine

The library might consider installing a materials dispensing machine, or MDM—sometimes called a vending jukebox or a book-lending machine. The MDM can hold a fairly large number of books, CDs, DVDs or some combination of material types depending on the size of the machine. The machines might be placed in a library itself (to reduce loss of materials), or where people congregate—shopping centers, subway platforms, and so forth. The machines can be set into a wall or built as a stand-alone kiosk. Cost of each machine is about $100,000. The return on investment is fairly quick and ranges from 12 to 24 months.

The Contra Costa County Library is the first in America to offer public library book-lending machines. Located at the Bay Area Rapid Transit's (BART) Pittsburg/Bay Point station, Library-a-Go-Go (the MDM) allows commuters with a Contra Costa County library card convenient access to library books. A second machine was installed at the El Cerrito Del Norte BART station (Community Digest 2009). Materials dispensing machines have also been installed inside a library. The Richmond (British Columbia, Canada) Public Library has installed two machines to dispense DVDs. Items are borrowed and returned directly to the machine. Interestingly, the dispensers' Web catalog gets more traffic than the library's main online catalog even though the machines contain less than 1 percent of the collection (Ellis 2008). The dispensers have virtually eliminated theft and handle the circulation cycle of 8,000 to 10,000 DVDs per month with reduced staff involvement.

Bookmobile

From the customer's perspective, a bookmobile eliminates the time and costs associated with travel to the closest library facility. Use of bookmobiles is limited but does present a viable alternative for delivering library services to a number of typically remote locations.

Most libraries with a bookmobile have developed criteria to determine the places and frequency the bookmobile will stop. Stops may be scheduled to meet targeted groups of individuals or simply smaller groups of people living some distance from the library. Bookmobiles have stopped at a variety of locations including:

- Migrant workers camps
- Primary schools with no library
- Head Start day care centers
- Other day care centers
- Senior centers
- Community centers
- Apartment buildings
- Trailer parks
- Housing projects
- Shopping centers
- Special events

Bookmobiles have a long history of service in the United States and other countries around the world and can be of varying sizes. Libraries in other countries have used horses, donkeys, mules, elephants, and camels to deliver library materials to rural locations.

The bookmobile might be a self-contained vehicle or a trailer (sometimes called a fifth-wheel) attached to a truck. The mobile collection typically contains popular adult and children's fiction and nonfiction materials. Materials from the other library facilities can usually be ordered and delivered on the next scheduled visit.

The primary disadvantage of a bookmobile is the short duration of each stop (30 minutes to a couple of hours) and the time between each visit. In addition, the limited space in the bookmobile severely limits the amount of materials that are accessible to anyone.

The bookmobile must be maintained on a regular basis and pass state safety inspections. Almost all bookmobiles return to their base of operations each day, although in some areas the bookmobile may stay out for a two- to three-day run. The bookmobile may be connected using wireless technology so that access to the library's automated library system (circulation and the online catalog) is provided. Dilger-Hill and MacCreaigh (2009), Clements (2008), Knight and Makin (2006), and Hawke and Jenks (2005) all provide an interesting discussion of the variety of issues confronting the delivery of library services using a bookmobile.

Print-On-Demand

When a customer is unable to locate a desired item on the shelf of a library they have several options:

- Request the item from another branch library using the online catalog

- Request the item from another library using interlibrary loan and wait several days (weeks) for the item

- Travel to another library or bookstore (not many people do)

- Determine if an eBook can be downloaded

- Give up (and many do)

Technology has recently offered a new alternative for libraries—namely, print-on-demand. The user can request that a copy of a book be printed assuming that copyright is not a concern and that an electronic copy of the book is available. The library can allow the customer to borrow and return the item, to purchase the item, or perhaps simply give the newly printed book to the customer. The consumables cost less than a penny a page so printing a 250 page perfect-bound book would cost about $2.50—ignoring the cost of the machine.

A commercial vendor, On Demand Books, has produced a stand-alone system called the Espresso Book Machine, which has been installed in two public libraries (as of May 1, 2011, the EBM is in the New Orleans (LA) Public Library, and the Riverside County (CA) Library System—the Temecula branch library). The EBM system has also been installed in university libraries, university bookstores, and private bookstores around the world. The primary disadvantage with the EBM is the initial purchase prince ($85,000 to $100,000) plus an additional $5,000 to $25,000 for a printer—price varies with speed and color options.

Users have access to several million electronic books (both in and out of copyright). Copyright costs for recently published books can be fairly reasonable (around $10 or less) so print on demand seems like an interesting way to deliver desired items without having to wait! Yet it is clear that for EBM to become successful, publishers must grant access to their copyright materials and provide the required digital files. Print on demand might also become a feasible alternative for interlibrary loan. Terri Geitgey (2011) and Kenning Arlitsch (2011) provide an interesting discussion about some of the impacts of installing an EBM.

Design of Facilities

Library after library has sacrificed reader accommodations to the imperatives of shelving. The crowding out of readers by reading materials is one of the most common and disturbing ironies in library space planning.
—Scott Bennett 2003

Many library users find the layout of collections and services to be a difficult, confusing, and often intimating place to navigate. Typically staff members are surprised with this statement and they expect a library customer to ask for help (at a service desk), understand the layout of the library, and to have plenty of time to enjoy all that the library has to offer! Yet many studies have demonstrated that people, especially men, do not ask for help, do not understand how to use a great many of the tools provided by the library, and typically spend only short periods of time in the library.

First impressions of a library and its usability are important. They ultimately affect whether people will return to the library time and again as people choose to use services that elicit feelings of comfort and pleasure. Remember that Zipf's Law of Least Effort is alive and well and operates in physical library spaces as well as online. Zipf's Law states that people tend to choose perceived ease of access over quality of content. This will increase frustration levels quickly since most library visitors do not understand library jargon, abbreviations, and acronyms. As floor plan complexity increases, wayfinding performance decreases. The combination of graphic and textual signs is most effective in reducing wayfinding errors—wrong turns, backtracking (O'Neill 1991).

Remember that the library has four basic components as shown in Figure 8.1 (McQuaid et al. 2003).

These components of the library experience include:

- **Customers**. The people who use the library. Keep in mind that they come in many "flavors" and there is no one single customer.

- **Organizers**. The way in which tools and systems organize the materials in a library's collections including:

  ° *Physical space* is the first organizer that people encounter. This includes the shelving and how it is organized, displays, tables and chairs, signage, size and shape of the service desks and so forth.

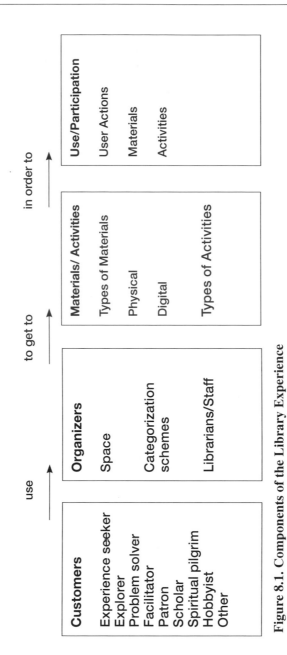

Figure 8.1. Components of the Library Experience

- ° *Organization schemes* include the library's catalog but also other tools including how the collection is organized (call number order, broad subjects, or some other method), pathfinders, lists, and so forth.

- ° *Librarians* and other staff members as well as friends who may be giving reader assistance advice, directions, or instruction.

- **Materials and services**. The reasons why people use the library. This component includes the library collections (physical and electronic) as well as the wide variety of services frequently offered by the library including story hours, instruction classes, programs, discussions, exhibits, speakers, films, and so forth.

- **Use/Participation**. The actual interaction with the materials and activities in the library or online. The most frequent use is the borrowing of materials and then these items are returned, placing a reserve (hold) for an item, attending a program, asking for research assistance, and so forth.

Customers have a wide variety of concerns and emotional responses as the result of attempting to use the library that includes: uncertain/confusion, fear, anxiety, annoyance, and, in some cases, delight and joy

Libraries must find ways to dramatically improve wayfinding for all users, especially library buildings that have multiple floors, which require reorientation in terms of layout since individual areas are rarely delimited or visually *'marked'* in a distinctive manner. This is especially true when various types of materials are stored on shelving that is uniform, despite type of media.

Envirosell, a retail store consulting firm owned and directed by Paco Underhill, has conducted a number of studies about how people navigate and what they do within a library facility. Studies have been conducted for the San Jose (CA) Public Library (Envirosell 2007a), the Hayward (CA) Public Library, the Los Angeles County Public Library [four large and five small branch facilities] (Envirosell 2007b), and the Metropolitan Library System [four Chicago area libraries] (Envirosell 2008).

Envirosell installs several video cameras and captures all of the movement by people within the library over a period of several days (more than 300 hours of video are recorded). Then a sample of users (typically between 200 and 300) entering the library are tracked and every place they stop is recorded on a map of the library—see Figure 8.2. In addition, a sample of several hundred people leaving the library are asked to participate in a brief interview about their planned and actual use of the library.

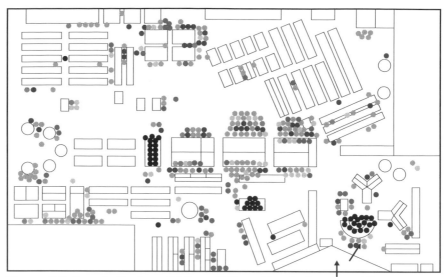

Figure 8.2. Sample Envirosell Map of Where People Stop in a Library

Among the consistent findings of the Envirosell studies across all of the libraries are:

- About a third of the customers visited the library to browse materials (split between books and audiovisuals).

- About a third of the customers had a specific item in mind.

- Slightly more than 60 percent of customers visit weekly or more frequently.

- Length of library visits varied by library—the average for some was under ten minutes while for others it was more than twenty minutes.

- A third of patrons visited a books section (use increases with age).

- Use of computers is more prevalent among younger (under thirty) customers.

- About half of the customers interact with staff in some way.

- More than two/thirds of customers borrow materials.

- Slightly more than ten percent view signage (it's invisible to most)

- Desk surfaces is not the best place for signage.

- Lounge areas work well when located near computers and periodicals.

- Three times as many customers browse audiovisual materials when it is located near the checkout area.
- Seventy percent don't know what titles they want when they walk in the door.
- Less than ten percent use the library catalog.
- About half of signage viewing is of stacks signage (is this signage the most user friendly?).
- Finding items on the shelf caused the greatest need for assistance.
- About a third of patrons wait in line (but not too long—an average of thirty seconds).

Envirosell recommendations included:

- Create a hierarchy of signage
  - ° Level one—Section identification (visible from the main path through the library)
  - ° Level two—Theme signage should be visible from outside the section in order to attract patrons
  - ° Level three—Call number identification
  - ° Level four—Shelf talk—use to direct readers to related titles
- Libraries are too cluttered with poor signage. Use odd shapes and sizes and create a sense of movement.
- Bring images into the space to create a more visually stimulating environment.
- Offer more ways to pair patrons with materials.
- Expand the audiovisual section.
- Change displays frequently
- Ethnic demographics of the community are not always reflected in the library's collection.

It would be possible to complete a similar study for your library using interior security cameras without hiring an expensive consulting firm.

Amenities

Coffee shops are now an integral part of many retail stores and many have suggested that libraries should provide space for such amenities. At the Botany

Downs Library in New Zealand you can purchase a glass of wine to sip while you read a magazine. Such a step calls into question libraries traditional aversion to allow food and drink (let alone beer and wine) into a library. However, this and other amenities can do much to make the library a more welcoming space. Many public libraries already provide a coffee shop and/or a gift shop. One important question to ask is: "Is sufficient space devoted to these amenities?"

Browse vs. Locate

A fundamental question that the managers of any public library should be asking themselves is, "How should the library be setup to best serve the interests of our customers?" Should we be relying on traditional high-density spine-out shelving or utilize more bookstore-like lower shelving that it designed to display books with the book covers visible? And another associated question is, "How should the library's nonfiction collection be organized?" Too often library management does not consider alternative ways of providing improved access to the materials in a library's collections. The reality is that most public library customers come to the library expecting to browse the collection to find items of interest while the library is set up using Dewey to support those who wish to search and do research.

In short, the fundamental questions are not about ditching Dewey or embracing the bookstore model but rather determining what is best for the community that the library serves. We can all learn from other alternative service delivery models and recognize that for many people Dewey is, in fact, daunting. It's about making things easier for the library's customer by being responsive to the needs of customers.

Organizing the Collection

For almost every public library in the world, the decision of how to organize a library's nonfiction collection is a no brainer—use the Dewey Decimal System. After all, more than 200,000 public libraries around the world do so and it's tradition! At the other end of the spectrum is the approach that bookstores use—no numbers! Just words! The bookstore standard is called BISAC—Book Industry Standards and Communications—that classifies books into 52 broad categories and each broad category can be further subdivided as needed. Rather than a hierarchical approach, BISAC uses an alphabetical list of categories ranging from Antiques to True Crime. The Open Shelves Classification is an open-source, crowd-sourced replacement for Dewey that was developed by *LibraryThing* members. And libraries that have combined BISAC and Dewy or BISAC and another classification system occupy the middle ground.

In a survey of public librarians, Barbara Fister (2009) found that the difficulty patrons have finding nonfiction is related to three factors: having trouble understanding the online catalog, feeling intimated by a classification system they don't understand, and wanting to go straight to the right shelf without having to look anything up. Not surprisingly, about one-fourth of the respondents thought enhancing Dewey with better signage was the solution. And almost one half felt that libraries should keep Dewey but add words to the call number. A few libraries have started to consider and implement alternatives to the Dewey-only traditional approach to organizing library collections. Among these libraries are:

- The Maricopa County (AZ) Library District customer surveys consistently revealed that 75 percent of customers came to the library to browse, not having a specific title or item in mind. The result was a decision to organize libraries the way the bookstores are organized to better meet customer needs. One of the important consequences of this decision was the need to abandon the Dewey Decimal System and to start labeling books using bookstore headings.

  The success of the Dewey-less library has more to do with the way the library is arranged, the clear and colorful signage, the furniture and shelving selected for the library. Due to the lower shelving height, the customer can see across the entire library and located related collections of materials. Related materials are grouped into "neighborhoods" and the neighborhoods are identified with large signs. Typically, materials are grouped together in U-shaped alcoves and comfortable chairs creating an atmosphere conducive to browsing. Within each neighborhood, books and DVDs are further divided into sections and subsections—from cooking to meditation, business to sports, and travel to families (Courtright 2010).

- The Darien (CT) Public Library opted to make that the entire nonfiction collection by being separated out into broad categories the library called "glades." Darien's glades include:
  - **Art and Literature**: Poetry, art, essays, writing, and literature
  - **Body and Soul**: Religion, philosophy, parenting, self-help, and health
  - **Finance**: Investing, personal finance, banking
  - **Home**: Cooking, gardening, decorating, and crafts
  - **Lives**: Biographies, memoirs
  - **Nature**: Animals, science, and math

- ° **Places**: Travel, language, travel writing
- ° **Technology**: technology
- ° **Times**: history
- ° **Work**: Economics, test preparation, accounting, marketing, college admissions.

The glades with the highest circulation per item are Places, Home, and Work. Rather than eliminating Dewey, Darien decided to place the glade name as a prefix to the call number in what is in effect a Dewey/bookstore mashup. Materials are organized in Dewey call number within each of the glades.

The library experienced more than a 500 percent increase in the circulation of picture books with the new glades organization of the collection! In the first year, circulation of the library's book collection increased by 47 percent while DVD circulation only increased by 20 percent (Caseroti and Ludwig 2010).

- The Frankfort (IL) Public Library District decided that they would "free Dewey" to provide greater accessibility to the library's nonfiction collection. The library participated in a study conducted by Envirosell (2008), a retail consulting firm, that identified patrons often come to the library without a specific title in mind and that there was little patron activity in the nonfiction collection. The library developed its own taxonomy using BISAC as the foundation and uses 56 Dewey Free subject taxonomies. Words and common terminology have been substituted for call numbers (McCoppin 2011). High circulating collections were moved closer to circulation and the entrance areas.

- The Rangeview (CO) Library District embarked on a reexamination of the assumptions and plans that were in place for the design and construction of four new branch library facilities. Perhaps the most visible sign of the "new" library was the decision to rebrand the library as "AnyThink."

- Rangeview implemented Dewey-less libraries in all of its branch libraries. Rangeview calls their unique BISAC-based subject headings "WordThink." Nonfiction materials are grouped into "neighborhoods" based on relationships to other neighborhoods and community being served. Shelves all have clear signage at the top of each unit. Materials are further sorted into smaller categories using shelf tags that protrude from the shelf (under cooking a customer might find vegetarian, ethnic foods, desserts, and so forth).

While the Southglenn branch of the Arapahoe (CO) Library District is still using Dewey, the collection is organized in "neighborhoods' based on lifestyle, subject, etc. So books on gardening and landscaping and building decks, which may not be in the same Dewey range, are shelved together. A total of twelve neighborhoods are used. The books are filed in Dewey order within the "neighborhoods." So the label on the spine indicates the Dewey number and also the neighborhood where the book belongs.

- The Schlessman branch of the Denver Public Library embraced merchandising of its collection by providing lots of audiovisual materials and tables stacked with popular materials. The merchandizing of its collection encourages customers to browse more and the use of attractive signage assists people in moving from one area to another. However, it is also important to note that the same model did not work as well in other neighborhoods with different demographics!

- The Brookdale branch of the Hennepin County Library took another approach. The library reduced its collection by 50 percent and organized the collection around subject areas called "information neighborhoods." These neighborhoods are marked by large retail-style signs that declare "Health & Fitness" or "Careers." Each neighborhood has its own unique carpet design so the customer will know they are in a new neighborhood. Each information neighborhood includes all the materials on the subject area—both circulating and reference. The one-stop approach makes things easier for the less-skilled user, which it is hoped will translate into a long-term relationship with the library.

- The Topeka and Shawnee County (KS) Public Library wanted to increase their use of their nonfiction collection. The library decided to organize their collection into neighborhoods, combining the best features of libraries and bookstores. The library has created three neighborhoods using signage to improve browsability. The Dewey numbers are maintained on each item. The results have been encouraging as evidenced by an increase in circulation and support from the community. Other neighborhoods are being planned with the goal of placing at least 60 percent of the nonfiction collection in a neighborhood.

- The Rakow branch of the Gail Borden (IL) Public Library District decided to organize its nonfiction collection into twenty-eight categories while its fiction collection is organized into ten categories.

Materials are displayed face out and signage is used to effectively assist the customer in identifying each section.

- The Westmont (IL) Public Library has gone Dewey free in its pre-reader area. The books are arranged by themes so that all the Dinosaur books are together, all the alphabet books are together, and so forth. Circulation of the pre-reader collection has increased 50 percent because the children can find their favorite topics.[1] The library is considering moving to Dewey free in its adult nonfiction collection.

- The Albany (NY) Public Library decided to embrace a Dewey-free approach in all of its branch libraries—the common name for a library collection classification system that uses words instead of numbers to categorize and organize nonfiction books. Dewey-free allows the library to group similar subjects together and make more natural selections for displaying complementary books.

- San Jose (CA) Public Library has eighteen branch libraries and a main library, which is a shared facility with the San Jose State University Library. The San Jose Public Library has embraced a new library design using a bookstore look and feel, while still responding to a wide range of needs. The library promotes wayfinding and self-navigating layouts for customer self-sufficiency. Sections in the library are branded using lighting, signage, colors, and shelving (merchandising) options. The service desk is de-emphasized as the first library experience through creative design. Staff is encouraged to build relationships with customers, moving away from the traditional transaction-based service model.

- The Richmond (British Columbia, Canada) Public Library serves a population of almost 200,000, of which 40 percent are of Asian heritage, with a main library and three branch facilities. The library has embraced merchandising of its collections and almost all of its materials are displayed face out using bookstore-like categories (with attractive signage) while preserving the use of Dewey. The result is extremely high per capita circulation rates (highest in Canada), use of self-help technology by the customers of the library, heavily used teaching and training technology center, and very popular programs (McNeely 2001).

- The Markham (Ontario, Canada) Public Library developed a "customer-centered classification" (C3) system. C3 replaces Dewey and assigns a 4-digital number (no decimals and no letters of the alphabet) to each BISAC subject grouping. C3 combines the best of the browsing-friendly bookstore with the ability to find a specific item quickly (without the need to rely on Dewey). All items are assigned a 4-digital classification number and a spine label reflecting this information is prepared. The library merchandizes all of its nonfiction collection and relies on colorful signage to indicate the subject groupings.

- And librarians at the Ethical Culture School in New York City devised a new categorization system called Metis that has 26 categories (using the A-Z letters of the alphabet). The result is that the children using the library have a greater success rate in finding books of interest.[2] The labels developed by the library are quite colorful and include a picture and a word.

Summary of Findings

Considering other alternatives to organizing a library's nonfiction collections with the traditional spine-out Dewey call number shelving allows a library to determine if there are other means of achieving the goal of improving access to the total library collections for its customers. The options can be considered along a continuum as shown in Figure 8.3

Implicit in the decision to utilize some of the alternatives is the need to reorganize the collection and move to display oriented, face-out merchandising of the collection. Some of the options combine the best of both worlds— the browser-friendly bookstore merchandising and finding specific items using a library classification system. Whether a library decides to adopt something similar to the Dewey/BISAC mashup used by the Darien Public Library, a new four-digit classification system (C3) developed by the Markham Public Library, or the words only BISAC system adapted and adopted by the Maricopa County Library System, the Anythink libraries, and the Frankfort Public Library among others, the end result is that customers are being better served by their library.

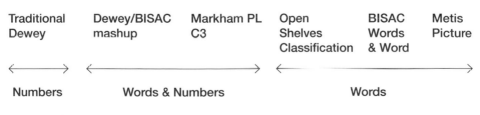

Traditional Dewey	Dewey/BISAC mashup	Markham PL C3	Open Shelves Classification	BISAC Words & Word	Metis Picture
Numbers	Words & Numbers			Words	

Figure 8.3. Classification Options

Take Action

Whether a library has branch facilities or not, there are a number of possible actions that should be considered. These include:

- Analyzing the use of each facility with an eye to the changing demographics of your community. A full-service branch facility may better serve the local community if it became a more specialized facility providing a more focused and narrower range of collections and services.

- The library may want to consider moving from the Dewey classification system to other options (ranging from a bookstore approach to an alternative classification system such as the C4 method developed by the Markham (Ontario, Canada) Public Library.

- The library may want to move from the use of traditional shelving to merchandising its collections.

- The library should consider adopting the use of out-of-the-box approaches to delivering access to collections including a print-on-demand service, use of materials dispensing machines (in shopping malls, commuter train stations, and so forth), and other options discussed in this chapter.

- Have several members of the management team track how people entering the library move about and use the facility. These individuals should then be approached and asked about their satisfaction with finding collections and services, the use of signs, and so forth. The objective should be to improve the wayfinding of the facility and to delight the customer.

Notes

1. Personal email from Christine Kuhn, director of the Westmont Public Library, on April 4, 2011.

2. For more information about Metis, visit the Web site http://metisinnovations.com/

Evaluating the Library

> *One of the great mistakes is to judge policies and*
> *programs by their intentions rather than their results.*
> —Milton Friedman

> *First get your facts; then you can distort them at*
> *your leisure.*
> —Mark Twain

An output is an end product of a service, in this case a library service, and implies a customer exposure to that service (physically or virtually). Broadly speaking, outcomes indicate the effect of this exposure in the life of the customer. It is also important to note that outcomes can be planned (sometimes called goals) or unintended, and that the actual outcomes may be less than, equal to, or greater than what was intended.

A framework or taxonomy for establishing the value that may arise from using library or information services was developed by Tefko Saracevic and Paul Kantor (1997a, 1997b). Using the vocabulary of users in responding to a questionnaire, Sarcevic and Kantor suggest that a customer has three potential reasons to use a library or information service: 1) to work on a task or project, 2) for personal reasons, or 3) to get an object, information, or perform an activity.

The authors also state that when a customer interacts with a library service that there are three areas of interaction that should be considered:

- **Resources**. There are three service aspects that are important to the customer:

  ° *Availability*. This traditional evaluation measure attempts to assess whether the library has the given resource, item, or service desired by the customer.

155

° *Accessibility.* This measure focuses on the ease with which the service can be accessed. Is a visit to the library required, for example?

° *Quality.* This measure assesses the degree to which a service or resource is accurate, current, timely, and complete.

- **Use of Resources, Services**. Library customers are interested in several perspectives:

  ° The degree of *convenience* in using the resource or service.

  ° *Ease of use.* How difficult is it to use a resource or library service?

  ° What *frustration*, if any, results from using the resource or library service?

  ° How *successful* is the customer in using a library service or resource?

  ° How much *effort* is required to move from one service to another? For example, performing a search to identify citations and then to retrieve the desired journal articles or other resources.

- **Operations and Environment**. Customers can be asked to rate the library and its services in four areas:

  ° How reasonable and clear are the library's *policies and procedures*? Do they facilitate access to the library's services or act as impediments?

  ° Are the *facilities* of adequate size? Does the physical layout and organization of the library resources facilitate access to the resources and services?

  ° Are library *staff members* helpful, efficient, and knowledgeable? Is there a clear understanding of the goals and objectives of the organization and a desire by library staff to offer a quality service?

  ° Assessing the performance of the *equipment* in the library. Is the equipment reliable and easy to use? Are user instructions or guides readily available?

But most importantly, Saracevic and Kantor focused on the results, outcomes, or the impact that a library or information service has directly on the individual and indirectly on the organization. These effects have been grouped into six categories:

- **Cognitive results**. Use of the library may have an impact on the mind of the customer. The intent of this category with this is to ask the question, "What was learned?" Thus, the customer may have:

   ° Refreshed memory of detail or facts

   ° Substantiated or reinforced knowledge or belief

   ° Provided new knowledge

   ° Change in viewpoint, outlook, perspective

   ° Getting ideas with a slightly different or tangential perspective (serendipity)

   ° Or, getting no ideas.

- **Affective results.** Use of the library or its services may influence or have an emotional impact on the customer. The customer may experience:

   ° A sense of accomplishment, success, or satisfaction

   ° A sense of confidence, reliability, and trust

   ° A sense of comfort, happiness, and good feelings

   ° A sense of failure

   ° A sense of frustration

- **Meeting expectations.** When using the library or an information service, the customer may:

   ° Be getting what they needed, sought, or expected

   ° Getting too much

   ° Getting nothing

   ° Have confidence in what they have received

   ° Receive more than expected

   ° Seek substitute sources or action if what they received did not meet expectations.

- **Accomplishments** in relation to tasks. As a result of using the library, the customer is:

   ° Able to make better informed decisions

   ° Achieve a higher quality performance

   ° Able to point to a course of action

   ° Proceeding to the next step

   ° Discovering people and/or other sources of information

   ° Improving a policy, procedure, and plan

- **Time aspects**. Some of the real value for the customer of a library is the fact that the information provided might lead to the savings of time in several possible ways. The customer may:
  - ° Save time as a result of using the service
  - ° Waste time as a result of using the service
  - ° Need to wait for service
  - ° Experience a service that ranges from slow to fast
  - ° Need time to understand how to use a service or resource
- **Money aspects**. Using the library or information service may, in some cases, clearly result in saving money or generating new revenues. The customer may be able to provide an:
  - ° Estimate of the dollar value of results obtained from a service or information received
  - ° Estimate of the amount of money saved due to the use of the service
  - ° Estimate of the cost in using the service
  - ° Estimate of what may be spent on a substitute service
  - ° Estimate of value (in dollars) lost where the service was not available or use was not successful

The process developed by Saracevic and Kantor, asking customers to reflect on their use of the library using a written survey, while comprehensive, is long and expensive to replicate. It should be noted that the first three results (cognitive, affective, and expectations) would normally translate in some way to having an impact on the latter three outcomes (accomplishments, time, and money).

When collecting evidence about the value of the public library to the community and its impact on people's lives, there are four primary roles that can be examined and reported:

- *Traditional functions*—reading and literacy, providing access to information leisure reading, and education
- *Social and caring roles*—including personal development, community empowerment and learning, local image, and social cohesion
- *Equity* between groups and communities as well as equity of access
- *Economic impact*—including business and employment information, training opportunities, and tourism information.

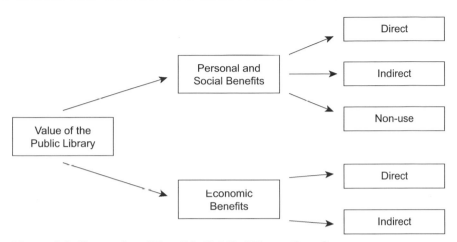

Figure 9.1. Categories of Possible Public Library Benefits

The various approaches to identify the value of a public library can be summarized in Figure 9.1. These approaches can be divided into two broad groups: economic and social.

There is also a tradition of not evaluating services provided by public-sector organizations for a variety of reasons. Fewer than 40 percent of municipal jurisdictions make any kind of meaningful use of performance measures in their management and decision processes. This, despite the fact, that when performance measures are actively embraced, service quality is improved, there is increased accountability of managers, and employees are more likely to focus on organizational goals (Poister and Streib 1999). However, as Osborne and Gaebler (1992) note, there are a number of consequences associated with a laissez-faire approach to performance measurement:

- What gets measured gets done.
- If results aren't measured, it is difficult to tell success from failure.
- If success can't be seen, it is difficult to reward it.
- If success is not rewarded, failure is either being ignored or rewarded.
- If success can't be seen, it is difficult to learn from it.
- If failure is not recognized, it can't be corrected.
- If results cannot be demonstrated, it is difficult to gain public support.

Of course, the problems of attempting to assess outcomes is complicated by the fact that the benefits from the use of the public library may accrue directly to the individual user, indirectly to the community, or both. In addition to the traditional use of input, process, and output measures, some researchers and public librarians have attempted to identify either the social benefits or economic benefits that occur as the result of using the local library. Yet, there are problems associated with the measurement of these benefits.

One very readable report, *Dividends: The Value of Public Libraries in Canada*, identified the many economic and social impacts of public libraries on Canadian society (Fitch and Warner 1998). Yet, the reader of *Dividends* is somewhat confused by the plethora of approaches that can be used to assert the value of the public library. The issue remains: how to choose?

The Library Brand

Respondents to the 2005 OCLC *Perceptions* survey clearly indicated that the library brand is "books." Unfortunately, the survey indicated that the "books" brand do not also stand for the intangible qualities of information familiarity, information trust, and information quality. The public library has not been successful in leveraging its brand to incorporate its growing investments in electronic resources and relevant Web-based services. Information consumers see libraries' role in the community:

> as a place to learn, as a place to read, as a place to make information freely available, as a place to support literacy, as a place to provide research support, as a place to provide free computer/ Internet access and more. (OCLC 2005, 6–8)

And five years later, the brand "Libraries = Books" was even stronger with support from 75 percent of the survey respondents (OCLC 2010). While individuals are devoting more and more time to online handheld devices, they are thinking about and spending less time at the public library. The most important role of the library remains "books, videos, and music."

Value of the Library to the Customer

One of the primary benefits that arise from the use of a library, especially in a corporate or governmental setting, is that individuals are able to save time (substitute librarian's time for the user's time). However, the value of time for public library users is something that must be ignored—even when the library user does save time as a result of a library visit. From the perspective of the public library, the community at-large is not able to benefit from this time saving for an individual user. And yet the public library does have a broad and positive economic impact on the community.

As a publicly funded organization, a public library embodies three economic concepts. These include:

- *Merit goods* are goods or services to which society accepts that everyone should have access, regardless of their means. Public libraries exhibit some merit properties since they help to maintain literacy, inform and empower citizens, stimulate the imagination, and so forth.

- A *public good* is one in which, even when consumed by another person, is still available for use by another. An item borrowed from the library's collection, once returned to the library, is available for use by another person.

- *External benefit* occurs when others, not directly involved in a transaction, nevertheless receives benefit form it. For example, a student uses the library to complete an assignment that leads to better grades, leads to graduation, and ultimately leads to a more qualified individual in the workforce. This individual is able to achieve higher career goals and rely less on government-provided support services.

A survey of library users in the state of Florida found support for the statements that public libraries (Fraser et al. 2002, McClure et al. 2001):

- Contributes to the prosperity of the local/state economy (91 percent agree or somewhat agree)

- Provides economic benefits to local businesses (82 percent agree or somewhat agree)

- Contributes to the financial well being of individuals (74 percent agree or somewhat agree).

These library users also felt that the presence of the public library helps attract new businesses to the community, the availability of library resources made them more productive at work, assists with issues concerning community development, and increased local property values. Yet, these are strictly the perceptions of patrons and library directors and do not represent a methodology that would actually calculate the actual benefits in terms of *dollars and cents*.

Generally, it is possible to separate the possible economic benefits that arise from a public library into two categories: direct and indirect benefits. Charles McClure and his colleagues have suggested that it is possible to think

Table 9.1. Matrix of Economic Benefits

Nature of Benefit	Class of Beneficiary		
	Individual	Local Business	Local Community
Direct	Specific economic benefits that accrue to the individual, e.g., cost of borrowing vs. buying materials	Specific economic benefits that accrue to local businesses, e.g., custom mailing lists	Specific economic benefits that accrue to the local community, e.g., tax base from library employment
Indirect	General economic benefits that accrue to the individual, e.g., increased property values	General economic benefits that accrue to local businesses, e.g., literate workforce	General economic benefits that accrue to the local community, e.g., quality of life factors

of a "matrix of economic benefits" that arise due to public libraries as shown in Table 9.1.

An alternative approach is to identify economic benefits using four different methodologies (Abend and McClure 1999):

- Cost-benefit analysis,

- Economic impact (contribution of actual dollars to the local community by the library),

- Subsidies the public library provides through its services to other organizations in the community, and

- Cost avoidance—a service provided by the public library need not be duplicated by other private or government agencies

Direct Benefits for the Individual

Possible direct economic benefits for an individual include the following:

- Savings from the non-purchase of books, magazines, newspapers, DVDs

- Information services to personal investors

- Technology access

- Health information

- Employment information and services

Savings from the Sharing Rather than Purchasing

The public library allows many individuals to share library resources reducing an individual's expenditures (and collectively the community's expenditures) on books, magazines, newspapers, audio, DVDs, and so forth. This frees up discretionary income for each library user to spend in other ways, and a portion will likely be spent in the local community.

One way to estimate this economic impact is to determine the average number and type of materials borrowed by an individual on an annual basis. This information, coupled with the average purchase price for each type of material (in the local community), would then result in an estimate of the savings that would accrue to the individual. However, it is likely that most people would not purchase all of the materials borrowed from the library if the library were no longer available.

Information Services to Personal Investors

Individuals wishing to make informed decisions about their investments can find a wealth of materials about investments at their local public library ranging from books, magazines, financial newsletters, and reports. Among the more popular financial publications are the *Wall Street Journal, Barons, Business Week, Value Line Investment Survey,* and many others. Few individuals can afford to subscribe to this variety of materials pertaining to personal financial planning and thus turn to the library for information about mutual funds, stocks, bonds, and other potential investments and portfolio management.

Technology Access

The public library can provide access to computers, printers, and the Internet. In addition, the library may offer classes so that individuals can learn new skills or enhance existing technology-related skills. It is not unusual for a library to offer classes pertaining to basic computer skills, email functions, word processing, spreadsheets, navigating the Internet, and use of Internet search engines.

This technology access is particularly important for a group within any community that cannot afford to purchase a computer or the monthly service charge to gain access to the Internet. Several studies have demonstrated that lower socioeconomic status is associated with lower levels of access to and use of computers and the Internet and is sometimes referred to as the "digital divide" (Bishop et al. 1999). Internet access is also of value to visitors in the community that may wish to check their email or perform other computer-based activities. As of January 2012, the Pew Internet Project indicated that 82 percent of Americans had access to the Internet at home and that broadband had reached 2/3rds of U.S. households (Rainie 2012).

A survey found that the "digital divide" between rich and poor children is rapidly shrinking as youngsters of all income levels and ethnic groups increasingly use the Internet (Corporation for Public Broadcasting 2003). Almost every public library provides access to computer-based technology and the Internet—an average of sixteen public access computers are available for use at each library (iPAC 2011). Yet, almost half of all libraries report that their Internet connection speeds are insufficient and that there is more demand for use of public access computers than libraries can currently provide. And with declining budgets, libraries are finding it challenging to maintain, let alone enhance, their information technology infrastructure.

Obviously providing such a service requires that the library have the necessary computer and communications network infrastructure in place. It also requires training staff to become knowledgeable in technology-related areas in order to teach classes, respond to questions, and resolve problems and so forth. Some libraries have found that using volunteers, as teachers/trainers, can be an effective alternative than relying solely upon library staff members.

Employment Information

The public library provides a wide range of information resources pertaining to résumés, developing interviewing skills, career requirements, civil service test requirements, and so forth. Some public libraries not only provide access to relevant materials but also provide programs that focus on practical information and developing skills that will be of value to the participants (Pankl 2001).

In addition to library materials related to employment and development of job skills, a large number of public libraries provide access to computers and the Internet. As such, an individual can prepare and update their résumé, look for job wanted listings, post a résumé at Internet job-related Web sites, and complete online fill-in-the-blank job applications.

Some libraries have established a dedicated area that provides resources and services to assist people in upgrading their skills and finding jobs (Eriksen and Maas 1997). A national survey of job and career centers located in public libraries found that people who availed themselves of the centers (Oserman and Durrance 1994):

- Had increased their understanding of the career possibilities

- Were able to make more informed decisions

- Took more positive steps to gain employment

- Gained self-esteem, and

• Developed new skills

Interestingly, Andrea Wadley and her colleagues suggested that public libraries are doing a poor job of reaching an important market segment—those who have jobs and are fully employed (Wadley et al. 1997a, 1997b). They suggested that the full-time employed are unable to utilize library services during the day and thus the hours the library is open, especially on the weekend, are very important to reaching this market segment.

Direct Benefits for Local Business

Possible direct economic benefits for local businesses include the following:

• Information services to local businesses
• Economic development

Information Services to Local Businesses

The public library will more than likely provide information resources and services that will be of interest to the self-employed in small or home-based businesses as well as to larger companies. The library may be the only affordable and available source of quality information for these individuals and organizations. The topical information sought by small businesses includes marketing (identification of potential customers), business plan development, technology, management skills, selling or motivation, and possible suppliers (Vaughn et al. 1996).

The information that is provided may be a response to a reference request, use, and circulation of business related periodicals, books, and reports. A wide range of information is used to ensure compliance with government regulations and procedures, developing a marketing plan, product development, creating a business plan, and so forth. Some public libraries develop specialized services for local businesses, which seem to engender real support (Ellis 1994).

The survey of users of the public library for business and career information, as noted in the *Counting on Results Project* report, found that the library was a source of information that was helpful in starting and developing a business (Lance et al. 2002)—see Table 9.2.

Another survey found that public libraries are used an average of seven times per year by professionals for work-related purposes (Griffiths and King 1994). And another survey of small business owners found that about one-third used the library frequently and were interested in finding information about consumer markets, technology, and management skills (Vaughn et al. 1996).

Table 9.2. Business & Career Information Outcomes

Outcomes	% Selected
Explored/started/developed a business	36
Developed job-related skills	31
Explored job/career or determined necessary education/ training	28
Made better investment or retirement decisions	26
Learned how to advance in job/career	15

Table 9.3. Sources of Information for Small Businesses

Sources	% Selected
Personal contacts (colleagues, friends, customers)	46
Magazines	30
Newspapers	13
Manufacturers	13
Organizations	9
Directories	8
Advertising	2
Libraries	2

Yet, for many other small business people, the library is not even on the radar screen as shown in Table 9.3 (Miele and Welch 1995).

Economic Development

The public library can become the hub or source of information about the community and the requirements for establishing a business or enterprise. The information may range from zoning regulations, availability of land or office space meeting certain requirements, availability of training programs, and so forth. In addition, the library's collection will contain information resources pertaining to starting a business, writing a business plan, creating a corporation, and so forth. In some cases, the library may create a specialized business reference service to provide more business-focused information services. Some libraries have developed a tier of business-related reference services in which a business or organization can pay for various levels of service of reference and on-demand information services. Small entrepreneurial business startups are an important segment of our economy and the public library can play an important role in the fostering of their success.

It is important to ensure that any specialized business-related service is not duplicating an existing publicly funded organization or service. Rather, it is recommended that the public library develop partnerships to assist with economic development activities with such organizations as the Chamber of Commerce, an economic development office, and so forth (Skrzeszewski and Cubberley 1997).

Direct Benefits for the Local Community

Possible direct economic benefits for the local community include the following:

- Employer
- Purchase of Goods and Services
- Retail Sales Due to the Library Being a "Destination."

Employer

The public library is an employer and providing jobs has a direct economic impact on the community. It can also be argued that some portion of the wages earned by the library staff members are spent in the local community and has a positive impact on the local economy. Sometimes this impact is called an "economic multiplier." For example, a dollar spent locally may generate "x" additional dollars in the local economy. Thus, a large portion of the public funds invested in the library are committed to employment and these dollars are "recycled" in the local economy.

Purchase of Goods and Services

Each year the library purchases materials to add to its collection. Some portion of these purchases may be made locally as opposed to using a national wholesaler. Additionally, the library will purchase goods and services nearby that support the local economy. While it occurs infrequently, the library may build a new building or expand an existing building. Such capital projects contribute to the local economy through employment and the purchase of building materials and services. The flip side of this approach is that most materials purchased for the library's collection are made using vendors that are not located locally.

Possible performance measures include: total value of purchases in the local community, number of local firms from which goods and services are purchased, and the value of construction and renovation of libraries.

Retail Sales

An economic-impact analysis is used to demonstrate the value that an institution has on the local or regional economy. Such an analysis starts with the fact that the institution attracts new dollars to the community. Such an analysis is typically used by a major museum or large library, e.g., the Art Institute of Chicago, the Natural History Museum of Chicago, the Museum of Modern Art in New York, the New York Public Library, the Library of Congress, and the Huntington Library in San Marino, CA. Such well-known institutions as these serve as a "destination" for visitors. While visiting the museum or large library, the visitors stay in area hotels, eat at local restaurants, and shop at various stores. The net effect is a boost to the local economy. In addition to the direct dollars spent by visitors, these dollars also cause the employment of other individuals. This spillover effect on the local economy is sometimes called the "multiplier effect."

The public library may be a "destination" or the reason for a trip from the home, school, or business. If so, an individual may combine the visit to the library with other activities, including shopping at nearby stores and restaurants. If library users are from outside the community and shop at nearby stores, this activity will benefit the local economy directly and potentially the tax base for the local jurisdiction in the form of increased sales tax revenues. In order to demonstrate the connection between use of the library and shopping at nearby stores, a survey must be conducted. It is important to demonstrate a cause-and-effect relationship between the library (the reason for the trip) and the shopping that was done at nearby stores and restaurants. In order to be effective, it must be demonstrated that the customer has a choice of where they can do their shopping and that the library attracts some nonresident individuals who combine shopping with a visit to the library.

Perhaps the most widely known economic impact study was prepared for the Seattle Public Library. A survey suggested that as much as 30 percent of the 2.5 million annual visitors to the library were from out-of-town (Berk & Associates 2005). The analysis suggested that these visitors spent $16 million annually in new spending in the downtown Seattle area (hotels, meals, car rentals, parking, ferries, and so forth). A similar economic impact study was prepared for the Carnegie Library of Pittsburgh (Carnegie Mellon University 2006).

A more recent study conducted on behalf of the Free Library of Philadelphia estimated the economic impact of the library to help Philadelphians learn to read and acquire working skills, locate job opportunities and develop career skills, develop or enhance their own businesses, and determine the increased value of neighborhood homes located near a branch public library (Fels Institute 2010). This study did not however determine the ROI for the library.

When the Hamilton Public Library in Ontario, Canada, introduced a non-resident user fee, the library experienced a reduction in the number of annual visits to the library to such an extent that parking revenues dropped more than was generated by the library's nonresident user fee (Roberts 1996). Another public library found that nonresident users of the library spent an average of $24 on each visit (Abend and McClure 1999).

Only some public libraries have the collections or other resources that serve as a destination for visitors. Thus, the economic-impact approach is one that is suited to partially demonstrating the value of the local public library and is likely applicable for only a few libraries.

Attracting Industrial/Commercial Development

Businesses wishing to locate in a community will look at a wide variety of factors including the availability of land/buildings to meet their needs, appropriate zoning, tax incentives from the local/state governments, a qualified labor force, proximity to markets and suppliers, as well as the quality of life in the community. In addition to the quality of schools, recreational and cultural opportunities, the availability of a high-quality public library plays an important role in assessing the quality of life (Lund 1986, Lyne 1988, Schmenner 1982, Sawyer 1996)). Given two or more sites where all other factors are equal, the perception of the quality of life in a community is often the deciding factor about where to locate a business. Robert McNulty (1988), a quality of life advocate, suggests that the "economics of amenity" will increase the economic value within a community. A good public library may be an important selling "point" for a community looking to attract retirees.

The difficulty with this approach to demonstrating the value of the public library is that rarely will the presence of a high-quality public library be the single factor in determining the quality of life for a community. Rather, the perception of the quality of life or a quality of life measure is based on a wide range of factors.

Cost-Benefit Analysis

A cost-benefit analysis can be prepared when the value of a product or service can be expressed in monetary terms and compared with cost. The cost-benefit methodology is routinely used to make financial investment decisions by corporations and it has also been used effectively to evaluate the benefits of education, local government services, social services, and environmental protection programs provided by nonprofit organizations, and government agencies.

There are five possible methods available to prepare a cost/benefit analysis and the different approaches can yield different results (King and Schrems 1978, Kingma 2001). The choice of the most appropriate cost/benefit analysis method depends on the situation. Four of these cost-benefit methodologies are designed to assist in making investment decisions and they include: maximize benefits for a given cost; minimize costs for a given level of benefits; maximize the net benefits; maximize the internal rate of return or return on investment (ROI). As such these methods are not appropriate for assessing the benefits of public library services and will not be discussed further in this book. Instead the focus of our attention is on an approach typically used to assess the value of all library services—identifing the ratio of benefits over costs.

Cost-benefit analysis suffers from a persistent and difficult problem. Usually the costs of a project or organization are clearly understood and occur in a very specific time period (a one-year budget cycle), while the benefits (which are much more difficult to quantify), are spread out over a longer period of time.

The process of this calculation is straightforward. All of the costs and benefits are identified. The ratio of benefits to costs, for example, $16 worth of benefits for every one dollar of costs or 16:1 is then determined.

A cost-benefit analysis can measure the direct benefits that accrue to those who have access to the services being measured. The library provides reading and information materials and services directly to its users. These users benefited directly from the use of those services and materials. The St. Louis Public Library tested the use of several cost-benefit methodologies to determine the best approach in valuing the direct benefits of use of the public library. While a range of benefit values were calculated, in general it was concluded that St. Louis Public Library users derived more than four dollars in benefits for each dollar spent (Holt and Elliott 1998, Holt et al. 1996, Holt et al. 1999).

An analysis of the various library ROI studies suggests that there are strengths and weaknesses with the various methodologies that have been used (Matthews 2011). Among the observations that can be made are:

Strengths

- The average return for most library ROI studies, four dollars to six dollars of benefits for every dollar expended, seems quite low but is consistent for many libraries

- Small libraries may have a higher ROI if the use of the library is considerably above average. That is, the library serves a larger population area than its "official" jurisdiction's area.

- Every ROI study has included the value of customer cost avoidance due to the borrowing of library materials and use of services.

However, there is wide variance in terms of how to establish the value of borrowing a book, DVD, CD, and so forth. Some libraries use retail price of a new book for example while others discount the retail price by some factor. Using a discount factor will lower the ROI but it is a more conservative approach.

- Using the economic impact of library spending in the community through the use of an economic model "multiplier" factor increases the ROI for the library.

Weaknesses

- The methodologies that have been used are several and quite varied.

- Valuing the time of the public that is saved due to library use results in higher ROI values but many decision makers find this problematical.

- Attempting to compare the ROI of one library to another is very problematical since the costs for a service will vary, often considerably, from one community to the next.

- Use of the contingent valuation methodology can result in fairly low estimates of value, as people are often quite unprepared to reflect on how to estimate the value of a service. This can result in quick snap judgments that provide fairly low estimates of value.

- Some city council persons, mayors, and city managers find the use of estimating the ROI for any municipal or county service to be problematical both from the perspective of the methodology that is used and are uncertain as to how to use the results of such studies.

Ultimately the library director must determine whether an economic analysis such as a cost-benefit analysis will strengthen the public library's position within the community and with the funding decision makers.

Due to their organized methods of identifying, locating and retrieving information, libraries save users millions of dollars each year in time not wasted in attempting to recreate data already available, time saved in not duplicating work already done and time not wasted on erroneous work.
—Robert Kraushaar and Barbara Beverly

Indirect Benefits for the Individual

Possible indirect economic benefits for an individual include enhanced property values.

Enhanced Property Values

The residential and commercial properties located near a public library facility may be a factor affecting the value of these properties. The positive impact on the valuation of these properties may then mean increased tax revenues for the local government (Cooper and Crouch 1994). The American Association of Certified Appraisers suggests that appraisers determine if a community has a local library when assessing property values. Obviously there are a large number of factors that affect the valuation of property and the proximity of a library will likely have both positive and negative components (increased traffic, parking). It might be possible to garner the testimonials from local real estate agents about the value of the library and nearby residential property values.

Indirect Benefits for Local Business

Potential indirect economic benefits for local business include a literate workforce.

Literate Workforce

Employers are seeking potential employees that are literate and motivated. In some cases, the availability of a wide range of reading materials promotes the goal of supporting "lifelong learning" among the citizens of a community. Given the rapid rate of change in our society in general and with technology in particular, it is important for people to upgrade their skills so that they can remain competitive in the marketplace. It is not surprising that a number of residents will turn to the public library for information resources as they pursue their goals of learning.

Indirect Benefits for the Local Community

Possible indirect economic benefits for the local community include the following:

- Literate workforce
- Workforce trained in using current information technology
- A population that is happy with their lives and where they live

One possible methodology that can be used to demonstrate the indirect economic benefits of a public library is to utilize a variation of the cost-benefit technique. The public library provides users with services from which the users receive direct benefits. And society as a whole receives an indirect benefit as the unemployed are hired; children grow up to be literate workers and informed citizens and so forth. Yet the value of these indirect benefits is very hard to identify and estimate. And without a fairly accurate of the benefits in quantifiable terms, the cost-benefit methodology cannot be used.

While some quality of life indexes (*Best Places to Live*, *Best Places to Retire*, *Southern California Best Places*, and so forth) use a "books per capita" statistic as one factor among many when rating communities, the reality is that a good quality public library has only a modest impact on the overall rating of a community. Other factors such as crime, recreational opportunities, weather, health, and the environment are much more important in the quality of life ratings are often "weighted" to reflect this higher value.

Indirect Benefits of Library Use

While almost everyone will acknowledge that library customers and the community itself benefits from the services provided by a public library, it is certainly impossible to calculate all of the economic benefits. These impossible to calculate benefits are known as indirect benefits or public benefits. Among the wide range of indirect benefits are leisure enjoyments, literacy encouragement for children and teens, library as place for community meetings, attending a program, and public access Internet computers.

Non-use Benefits

In addition to use value, economists have recognized that individuals, who make no use of a public good, such as a public library, might derive satisfaction from its mere existence. The literature discussing this concept in the cultural arena has called non-use value a variety of other names—existence value, bequest value, vicarious consumption, prestige value, education value, option value, and several others (Aabo 2005). The non-use value of a public library can be considered as the utility individuals obtain from libraries other than their active use of a library. Non-use value or benefits can be grouped into two categories: that it will be a benefit to an individual at some time in the future and that it is of benefit to others in the community now and in the future. Altruistic motivations, defined as concern for poor people, people of color, children, and others who have access to the broad range of services provided by the public library, are likely to be considered when someone is asked to reflect on the value of public libraries. There is a willingness of individuals to support the library so that others may benefit and it is appreciated and valued as an institution that improves the quality of life in the community.

Non-use benefits are difficult to quantify and if measured, are open to considerable debate. While contingent valuation has been used in some studies to determine non-use benefits, many ROI studies ignore the value of non-use in an attempt to calculate conservative return on investment numbers.

Summary of Findings

Clearly there is no shortage of tools to estimate the value of using the public library. The principal challenge that arises is for the library to select one or more tools that will resonate with the stakeholders of their particular community. It is important when attempting to establish the value of the library to clearly identify the direct, indirect, and non-use benefits that arise from the library. And more importantly, it is important to create a variety of ways to communicate the value of the library to key community stakeholders.

Take Action

Identifying and communicating the value of the library is becoming more important compared to ten to 15 years ago. Among the actions a library might take are:

- Try to identify the benefits that arise from a wide variety of library services and collections. It may or may not be possible to quantify each of these benefits but the real value for the library director and the management team to go through this exercise is to have a better idea of how value only occurs in the life of an individual from the interaction with one or more items in a collection or interaction with a library staff member.

- Try to identify the direct and indirect benefits for a group of library customers—parents attending a story time for very young children; homework assistance for elementary, middle school, and high school students; entrepreneurs attempting to start a business; people wanting to learn more about computer technology and software skills; improving the likelihood of getting a job by learning how to create or polish a resume, interviewing skills; and so forth.

- Create a cost-benefit analysis by identifying the value of each library service in your community and then each value by the amount of use. The total value of the use equals the benefits for the library. Divide the benefits by the library's annual operating budget to derive the cost-benefit ratio (also known as the Return on Investment).

- If you believe that your brand is more than books, how are you marketing to people in your community about the wide range of collection materials and services that people might avail for themselves? What is the library's value proposition? How does your library add value in the life of each customer? What is your library's brand?

References

Aabo, Svanhild. "Valuation of Public Libraries," in *New Frontiers in Public Library Research*. Carl Johannsen and Leif Kajbrg (Editors). Lanham, MD: Scarecrow Press, 2005, 97–109.

Aabo, Svanhild, and Ragnar Audunson. "Rational Choice and Valuation of Public Libraries: Can Economic Models for Evaluating Non-Market Goods be Applied to Public Libraries?" *Journal of Librarianship and Information Science*, 34 (1), March 2002, 5–15.

AAP. *BookStats2011*. New York: American Association of Publishers, 2011. Available at http://www.publishers.org/resources/

Abend, Jennifer, and Charles R. McClure. "Recent Views on Identifying Impacts from Public Libraries." *Public Library Quarterly*, 17 (3), 1999, 3–29.

Albanese, Andrew. "Survey Says Library Users Are Your Best Customers." *Publishers Weekly*, October 28, 2011.

American Library Association. *EBook Business Models for Public Libraries*. Chicago: ALA, August 8, 2012. Available at http://americanlibrariesmagazine.org/sites/default/files/EbookBusinessModelsPublicLibs_ALA.pdf

American Library Association. @ *your library: Attitudes Toward Public Libraries Survey*. Chicago: ALA, 2002. Available at http://www.sos.wa.gov/library/libraries/projects/outreach/docs/2002_ALA_Attitudes.pdf

Anderson, Chris. "In the Next Industrial Revolution, Atoms Are the New Bits." *Wired*, 18 (2), February 2010. Available at http://www.wired.com/magazine/2010/01/ff_newrevolution/all/

Anderson, Chris. *The Long Tail: Why the Future of Business is Selling More of Less*. New York: Hyperion Press, 2006.

Anthony, Robert. *Management Control Systems*. Homewood, IL: Richard D. Irwin, 1965, 4.

Arlitsch, Kenning. "The Espresso Book Machine: A Change Agent for Libraries." *Library HiTech*, 29 (1), 2011, 62–72.

Augustine, Susan, and Courtney Greene. "Discovering How Students Search a Library Web Site: A Usability Case Study." *College & Research Libraries*, 63 (4), July 2002, 354–65.

Ballard, Terry, and Anna Blaine. "User-search limiting behavior in online catalogs." *New Library World*, 112 (5/6), 2011, 261–273.

Ballard, Thomas. *The Failure of Resource Sharing in Public Libraries and Alternative Strategies for Service*. Chicago: American Library Association, 1986.

Barrett, Richard. *Liberating the Corporate Soul*. Boston: Butterworth Heinmann, 1998.

Bartlett, Wendy. "Floating down the Cuyahoga." *Public Libraries*, May/June 2012, 51 (3), 15.

Beers, G. Kylene. "No Time, No Interest, No Way!" *School Library Journal*, 42 (20, February 1996, 110–114.

Bennett, Scott. *Libraries Designed for Learning*. Washington, DC: Council on Library and Information Resources, 2003.

Berk & Associates. *The Seattle Public Library Central Library: Economic Benefits Assessment. The Transformative Power of a Library to Redefine Learning, Community, and Economic Development*. Seattle: Berk & Associates, 2005. Available at http://www.berkandassociates.com/pdf/Draft Report.pdf

Besen, Stanley, and Sheila Kirby. *eBooks and Libraries: An Economic Perspective*. Chicago: American Library Association, September 2012. Available at http://www.ala.org/offices/sites/ala.org.offices/files/content/oitp/publications/booksstudies/ebooks_libraries_economic_perspective.pdf

Bishop, Ann P., Tonyia J. Tidline, Susan Shoemaker, and Pamela Salela. "Public Libraries and Networked Information Services in Low-Income Communities." *Libraries & Information Science Research*, 21 (3), 1999, 361–90.

Boekesteijn, Erik. "Discover Innovations at DOK, Holland's 'Library concept Center." *Marketing Library Services*, 22 (2), March/April 2008, 1–4.

Borgman, Christine. "Why are online catalogs still hard to use?" *Journal of the American Society for Information Science,* 47 (7), July 1996, 493–503.

Brantley, Steve, Annie Armstrong, and Krystal Lewis. "Usability Testing of a Customizable Library Web Portal." *College & Research Libraries*, 67 (3), March 2006, 146–63.

Bray, Honore, and Gloria Langstaff. "Does it matter where the books are shelved (floating collections)." *PNLA Quarterly*, 72 (1), Fall 2007, 19–20.

Breeding, Marshall. *Knowledge Based and Link Resolver Study: General Findings*. Stockholm, Sweden: The National Library of Sweden, 2012. Available at http://www.kb.se/dokument/Knowledgebase_linkresolver_study.pdf

Breeding, Marshall. "A Use Statistic for Collection Management: The 80/20 rule Revisited." *Library Acquisitions: Practice & Theory*, 14, 1990, 183–189.

Buckland, Michael K. *Book Availability and the Library User*. New York: Pergamon, 1975.

Bucknell, Terry. "Garbage In, Gospel Out: Twelve Reasons Why Librarians Should Not Accept Cost-per-Download Figures at Face Value." *The Serials Librarian*, 63 (2), 2012, 192–212.

Burke, Susan. "Public Library Resources Used by Immigrant Households." *Public Libraries*, July/August 2008, 32–41

Calvert, Philip, and Rowena Cullen. "Further Dimensions of Public Library Effectiveness II: The Second Stage of the New Zealand Study." *Library and Information Science Research*, 16 (2), Spring 1994, 87–104.

Canty, Adrienne Brown, et al. "Floating Collections at the Edmonton Public Library." *Evidence Based Library and Information Practice*, 2012, 7 (1), 65–69.

Carnegie Mellon University. *Carnegie Library of Pittsburgh: Community Impact and Benefits*. Pittsburgh, PA: Carnegie Mellon University, Center for Economic Development, April 2006.

Caseroti, Gretchen, and Sarah Ludwig. "Dewey-Lite. In Perspectives: Dewey or Don't We?" Nanci Milone Hill (Editor). *Public Libraries*, July/August 2010, 14–20.

Change, Pao-Long, and Pao-Nuan Hsieh. "Customer Involvement with Services in Public Libraries." *Asian Libraries*, 6 (3/4), 1997, 242–49.

Charan, R., and G. Colvin. "Why CEOs Fail." *Fortune*, 139, June 21, 1999, 68–78.

Cherry, Katie, Kay Drache, Phil Feilmeyer, Elizabeth Feinberg, Cathy Fischer, Judith Friedrich, Jackie Gillespie, and Sarajo Wentling. *Collection Handling Action Team Report*. Minnetonka, MN: Hennepin County Library, 2004. Available from www.hclib.org/extranet/CHATFinalRpt7.0mgc.pdf

Chevalier, Judith, and Dina Mayzlin. *The Effect of Word of Mouth on Sales: Online Book Reviews*. Working Paper 10148. Cambridge, MA: National Bureau of Economic Research, December 2003.

Chen, Ching-chih, and Peter Hernon. "Library Effectiveness In Meeting Information Consumer's Needs" in *Library Effectiveness: A State Of The Art*. Papers from a 1980 ALA Preconference, June 27 & 28, 1980, New York, NY. Chicago: American Library Association, 1980, 49–63.

Chia, Christopher. "Transformation of Libraries in Singapore." *Library Review*, 50 (7/8), 2001, 343–48.

Ciliberti, Anne, Marie Radford, Gary Radford, and Terry Ballard. "Empty Handed? A Material Availability Study and Transaction Log Analysis Verification." *The Journal of Academic Librarianship*, 59, July 1998, 282–89.

Ciliberti, Anne, Mary Casserly, Judy Hegg, and Eugene Mitchell. "Material Availability: A Study of Academic Library Performance." *College & Research Libraries*, 48, November 1987, 513–27.

Circle, Alison, and Kerry Bierman. "How Giving Up Many Brands in Exchange for One Created a Marketing Plan with Big Impact." *Library Journal*, 134 (11), June 15, 2009, 32–35.

Clark, Philip. "Patterns of Consistent, Persistent Borrowing Behavior by High Intensity Users of a Public Library." *Public Libraries*, 37 (5), September/October 1998, 298–301.

Clements, Angela. "On the Move with the TCPL Mobile Library: What It Takes to Keep Rolling." *Indiana Libraries*, 27 (1), 2008, 26–32.

CLIR. *Collections, Content, and the Web*. Publication #88. Washington, DC: Council on Library Resources, 2000.

Collins, Jim. *Leader to Leader*. San Francisco: Jossey-Bass, 1999.

Collins, Mary A., and Kathryn Chandler. *Use of Public Library Services by Households in the United States: 1996*. NCES 97–446. Washington, DC: U.S. Department of Education, Office of Educational Research and Improvement, 1997.

Community Digest. *Oakland Tribune*, June 16, 2009, 34.

Connaway, Lynn Silipigni, Timothy Dickey, and Marie Radford. "If It Is Too Inconvenient, I'm Not Going After It: Convenienience as a Critical Factor in Information-Seeking Behaviors." *Library and Information Science Research*, 33, 2011, 179–190.

Cooper, Jeffrey M., and Marilyn C. Crouch. "Benefit Assessment Helps Open Doors Of One Cash-Strapped California Library." *American Libraries*, 25, March 1994, 232–234.

The Corporation for Public Broadcasting. *Connected To The Future: A Report On Children's Internet Use For The Corporation for Public Broadcasting*. Washington, DC: The Corporation for Public Broadcasting, 2003.

Courtright, Harry. "The National Impact of the Dewey-Less Library. In Perspectives: Dewey or Don't We?" Nanci Milone Hill (Editor). *Public Libraries*, July/August 2010, 14–20.

Craven, Jenny, Frances Johnson, and Geoff Butters. "The Usability and Functionality of an Online Catalogue." *Aslib Proceedings*, 62 (1), 2010, 70–84.

Cress, Ann, Kathy Hallaron, Kathy Munch. *Floating Collections—Is It Time For Your Library to Convert?* Presentation at the CAL Conference, November 9, 2007. Available at www.cal-webs.org/handouts07/Floating.ppt

Cropper, Dale. "Floating Collections: More Freshness, Less Staff Time." *Public Libraries*, May/June 2012, 51 (3), 19–20.

Cullen, Rowena, and Philip Calvert. "Further Dimensions of Public Library Effectiveness: Report on a Parallel New Zealand Study." *Library and Information Science Research*, 15 (2), Spring 1993, 143–64.

Deane, Gary. "Bridging the Value Gap: Getting Past Professional Values to Customer Value in the Public Library." *Public Libraries*, September/October 2003, 315–19.

D'Elia, George, and Eleanor J. Rodger. "Public Library Roles and Patron Use: Why Patrons Use the Library." *Public Libraries*, 33 (3), 1994, 135–44.

D'Elia, George. "The Development and Testing of a Conceptual Model of Public Library User Behavior." *Library Quarterly*, 50, 1980, 410–30.

D'Elia, George, Corinne Jorgensen, Joseph Woelfel, and Eleanor Jo Rodger. "The Impact of the Internet on Public Library Use: An Analysis of the Current Consumer Market for Library and Internet Services." *Journal of the American Society for Information Science and Technology*, 53 (10), 2002, 802–820.

Delin, Catherine, Peter Delin, and Laura Cram. "Patterns and Preferences in Recreational Reading." *Australian Library Journal*, 44 (3), August 1995, 119–131.

Dempsey, Beth. "Designing Buildings and Services from the End User's Viewpoint Transforms Access for Everyone." *Library Journal*, 130 (20), December 15, 2005, 72–75.

Dempsey, Lorcan. "Thirteen Ways of Looking at Libraries, Discovery, and the Catalog: Scale, Workflow, Attention." *Educause Review Online*, December 10, 2012. Availale at http://www.educause.edu/ero/article/thirteen-ways-looking-libraries-discovery-and-catalog-scale-workflow-attention

Dempsey, Lorcan. "Always On: Libraries in a World of Permanent Connectivity." *First Monday*, 14 (1–5), January 2009.

Dereli, Cynthia. "Strategy and Strategic Decision-Making in the Smaller Local Authority." *International Journal of Public Sector Management*, 16 (4), 2003, 25–60.

Dervin, Brenda, and Benson Fraser. *How Libraries Help*. California: University of the Pacific, 1985.

Dilger-Hill, Jeannie, and Erica MacCreaigh. *On the Road with Outreach: Mobile Library Services*. Santa Barbara: Libraries Unlimited, 2009.

Drucker, Peter F. *Management: Tasks, Responsibilities and Practice*. New York: Harper & Row, 1973, 125.

Drucker, Peter. *Management: Tasks, Responsibilities, Practices*. New York: Butterworth-Heinemann, 1988, 68.

Drucker, Peter. *Managing the Non-Profit Organization*. New York: HarperBusiness, 1990, 5.

Dutton, William, and Grant Blank. *Next Generation Users: The Internet in Britian. Oxford Interent Survey 2011*. Oxford: University of Oxford, 2011.

Eisenhardt, Kathleen. "Strategy as Strategic Decision Making." *Sloan Management Review,* 40 (3), Spring 1999, 66.

Elliott, Donald S., Glen E. Holt, Sterling W. Hayden, and Leslie E. Holt. *Measuring Your Library's Value: How to Do a Cost-Benefit Analysis for Your Public Library*. Chicago: American Library Association, 2007.

Ellis, Kem B. "The Challenge of Measuring the Economic Impact of Public Library Service." *North Carolina Libraries,* 52, Summer 1994, 52–56.

Ellis, Mark. "Dispensing with the DVD Circulation Dilemma." *Computers in Libraries*, February 2008, 11–14.

Enis, Matt. "Accessibility Upgrade: EPUB, Libraries, and Ebook Accessibility." *Library Journal*, 138 (7), April 15, 2013, 31–33.

Enis, Matt. "DVD Circ Holds Steady." *Library Journal*, 137 (19), November 15, 2012, 38–40.

Enis, Matt. "Mobile Evolution: How Apps Are Adapting to a New Device Ecosysstem." *Library Journal*, 138 (3), February 15, 2013. 42–45.

Envirosell. *Envirosell Final Report for the Metropolitan Library System*. New York: Envirosell, April 29, 2008.

Envirosell. *Envirosell Presents County of Los Angels Public Library Study*. New York: Envirosell, February 16, 2007b.

Envirosell. *San Jose Public Libraries and Hayward Public Libraries: Final Report*. New York: Envirosell, February 16, 2007a. Available at http://www.sjpl.org/sites/all/files/userfiles/SVPL-HPL_final_report.pdf

Eriksen, Norman J., and Jan A. Maas. "Serving the Patron through Referral Lists: The Brooklyn Experience." *Journal of Interlibrary Loan, Document Delivery & Information Supply*, 7 (4), 1997, 49–58.

Fast, Karl, and Grant Campbell. "'I Still Like Google': University Student Perceptions of Searching OPACs and the Web." *Proceedings of the 67th ASIS&T Annual Meeting*, 41, 2004, 138–146.

Fels Institute of Government. *The Economic Value of the Free Library of Philadelphia*. Philadelphia: The University of Pennsylvania, Fels Institute of Government, October 2010. Available at http://www.freelibrary.org/about/Fels_Report.pdf

Finlay, Joel. "The Strategic Visioning Process." *Public Administration Quarterly*, 18 (1), Spring 1994, 64–74.

Fister, Barbara. "The Dewey Dilemma." *Library Journal*, 134 (16), October 1, 2009, 22–25.

Fitch, Leslie, and Jody Warner. "Dividends: The Value of Public Libraries in Canada." *The Bottom Line*, 11 (4), 1998, 158–79.

Fitzgerald, Scott F. "The Crack-Up." 1936, as noted in *Bartlett's Familiar Quotations*.

Franklin, William, Marc Lambert, Brian Light, Eileen Mendez, and Nancy Redfield. *Report on Issues Regarding Possible Implementation of Floating Collections in the Contra Costa Library*. 2005. Available at www.ccclib.org/libinfor/Commission/Meetings/2005/May/doggedretrievers final.pdf

Fraser, Bruce T., Timothy W. Nelson, and Charles R. McClure. "Describing the Economic Impacts and Benefits of Florida Public Libraries: Findings and Methodological Applications for Future Work." *Library & Information Science Research*, 24 (3), 2002, 211–33.

Futterman, Marc, and Judy Michaelson. "Data Rules: How Mapping Technology Drives Better Customer Service." *Public Library Quarterly*, 31 (2), 2012, 141–152

Galbi, Douglas. "Book Circulation Per U.S. Public Library User Since 1856." *Public Library Quarterly*, 27 (4), 2008, 351–371.

Geitgey, Terri. "The University of Michigan Library Espresso Book Machine Experience." *Library HiTech*, 29 (1), 2011, 51–61.

Ginsky, Andrea. "Jumping In and Learning to Float." *Public Libraries*, May/June 2012, 51 (3), 17–19.

Godin, Seth. "The Future of the Library." *Seth Godin's blog*, 2011. Available at http://sethgodin.typepad.com/seths_blog/2011/05/the-future-of-the -library.html

Goldberg, B. "Statistics on Renewals in Public Libraries." *Public Library Quarterly*, 10 (2), 1990, 63–68.

Gorman, Michael. "Values of Steel in Thirty Days." *American Libraries*, 31 (4), April 2000, 39.

Green, Steven. "Rational Choice Theory: An Overview." TX: Baylor University, May 2002. Available at http:// business.baylor.edu/steve_green/green1.doc

Griffiths, Jose-Marie, and Donald King. "Libraries: The Undiscovered National Resource," in *The Value And Impact Of Information*, M. Feeney and M. Grieves (Eds.). London: Bowker & Saur, 1994, 79–116.

Guajardo, Richard, and Rachel Vacek. *Web-Scale Discovery: Post Implementation*. A presentation at the Texas Library Association Conference, Houston, Texas, April 20, 2012. Available at http://www.slideshare.net/vacekrae/ webscale-discovery-post-implementation

Guernsey, Lisa. "Are eBooks Any Good?" *School Library Journal*, June 1, 2011.

Haley, R.I. "Benefit Segmentation: A Decision Oriented Research Tool." *Journal of Marketing*, 32, July 1968, 30–35.

Hawke, Bernie, and Fiona Jenks. "On the Move: Mobile Library Services in New Zealand." *Australasian Public Library and Information Services*, 18 (3), September 2005, 93–105.

Heritage Canada. *Reading and Buying Books for Pleasure: 2005 National Survey Final Report.* Montreal: Heritage Canada, March 2005.

Hernon, Peter, and Joseph Matthews. *Reflecting on the Future: Academic and Public Libraries.* Chicago: ALA Editions, 2013.

Hernon, Peter, and Joseph Matthews. *Listening to the Customer.* Santa Barbara, CA: Libraries Unlimited, 2011.

Hoffert, Barbara. "Materials Mix." *Library Journal*, 138 (3), February 15, 2013, 26–28.

Hoffman, Melissa, and Sharon Yang. "How Next-Gen R U? A Review of Academic OPACs in the United States and Canada." *Information Today*, July/ August 2011, 26–29.

Holt, Glen, and Donald Elliott. "Proving Your Library's Worth: A Test Case." *Library Journal*, 123 (18), November 1998, 42–44.

Holt, Glen, Donald Elliott, and Amonia Moore. "Placing a Value on Public Library Services. A St. Louis Case Study." *Public Libraries*, 38 (2), March-April 1999, 98+.

Holt, Glen, Donald Elliott, and Christopher Dussold. "A Framework for Evaluating Public Investment in Urban Libraries." *The Bottom Line*, 9 (4), Summer 1996, 4–13.

Houghton, Sarah. "I'm Breaking Up with eBooks (and You Can Too)." *Librarian in Black* blog. August 1, 2012. Available at http://librarianinblack.net/librarianinblack/2012/08/ebookssuckitude.html

Houghton, Sarah. "The eBook User's Bill of Rights." *The Librarian In Black* blog. February 28, 2011. Available at http://librarianinblack.net/librarianinblack/2011/02/ebookrights.html

Howe, Jeff. *Crowdsourcing: Why the Power of the Crowd is Driving the Future of Business*. New York: Random House, 2008.

IFLA. *IFLA and Library eLending*. The Hague: International Federation of Library Associations, 2013. Available at http://www.ifla.org/files/assets/clm/publications/ifla-background-paper-e-lending-en.pdf

Institute for Learning Innovation. *Dover, DE Library User Identity—Motivation Pilot Study*. Dover, DE: Delaware Division of Libraries, December 2005.

iPAC. *2010–2011 Public Library Funding and Technology Access Survey: Survey Findings and Results*. College Park, MD: University of Maryland, Information Policy & Access Center, June 21, 2011.

Irvine, Ann. "Is Centralized Collection Development Better? The Results of a Survey." *Public Libraries*, 34 (4), July/August 1995, 216–19.

Ithaka S+R. *Faculty Study 2009: Key Strategic Insights for Libraries, Publishers, and Societies*. New York. Ithaka, 2010. Available at http://www.sr.ithaka.org/research-publications/faculty-survey-2009

Japzon, Andrea, and Hongmian Gong. "A Neighborhood Analysis of Public Library Use in New York City." *Library Quarterly*, 75 (4), 2005, 446–463.

Joeckel, Carleton, and Leon Carnovsky. *A Metropolitan Library in Action: A Survey of the Chicago Public Library*. Chicago: University of Chicago Press, 1940.

Johal, Jinder, and Thomas Quigley. "Six Years of Floating Collections: The Vancouver Exeprience." *Public Libraries*, May/June 2012, 51 (3), 13–14.

Kantor, Paul. "The Library as an Information Utility in the University Context: Evaluation and Measurement of Services." *Journal of the American Society of Information Science*, 27, 1976, 100–112.

Kantor, Paul. "Demand-Adjusted Shelf Availability Parameters." *The Journal of Academic Librarianship*, 7 (2), 1981, 78–82.

Kantor, Paul. *Objective Performance Measures for Academic and Research Libraries*. Washington, DC: Association of Research Libraries, 1984.

Kaplan, Sarah, and Eric D. Beinhocker. "The Real Value of Strategic Planning." *MIT Sloan Management Review*, 44 (2), Winter 2003, 71–76.

Kasperek, Sheila, Erin Dorney, Beth Williams, and Michael O'Brien. "A Use of Space: The Unintended Messages of Academic Library Web Sites." *Journal of Web Librarianship,* 5, 2011, 220–248.

Kelley, Michael. "A Toolkit for Taking Stock: Libraries Leverage New Metrics Driven by Data from CollectionHQ." *Library Journal*, September 17, 2012,

Keng, Kau Ah, Kwon Jung, and Jochen Wirtz. "Segmentation of Library Visitors in Singapore: Learning and Reading Related Lifestyles." *Library Management*, 24 (1/2), 2003, 20–33.

Kenney, Brian. "Imagine This." *School Library Journal*, December 2005, 55.

Kiechel, Walter. "Corporate Strategists Under Fire." *Fortune*, 106, December 27, 1982, 34–39.

King, John L., and Edward L. Schrems. "Cost-Benefit Analysis of Information Systems Development and Operation." *Computing Surveys*, 10 (1), March 1978, 22–34.

Kingma, Bruce R. *The Economics of Information: A Guide to Economic and Cost-Benefit Analysis for Information Professionals*. Englewood, CO: Libraries Unlimited, 2001.

Knauft, E.B., Renee Berger, and Sandra Gray. *Profiles of Excellence*. San Francisco: Jossey-Bass, 1991.

Knight, Robert, and Lynne Makin. "Branches on Wheels: Innovations in Public Library Mobile Services." *Australasian Public Library and Information Services,* 19 (2), June 2006, 89–96.

Koontz, Christine. "A History of Location of U.S. Public Libraries Within Community Place and Space: Evolving Implications for the Library's Mission of Equitable Space." *Public Library Quarterly*, 26 (1/2), 2007, 75–100.

Koontz, Christine. *Library Siting and Location Handbook*. Westport, CT: Greenwood Press, 1997.

Koontz, Christine. "Public library site evaluation and location: Past and present market-based modeling tools for the future." *Library and Information Science Research*, 14 (4), 1992, 379–409.

Koontz, Christine. "Technology—Pied Piper or playground bully, or Creating meaningful measures using emerging technologies: Separating the reality from the myths." *Proceedings of the 4th Northumbria International Conference on Performance Measurement & Libraries & Information Services.* New Castle, England: University of Northumbria, 2001.

Kopczynski, Mary, and Michael Lombardo. "Comparative performance measurement: Insights and lessons learned from a consortium effort." *Public Administration Review*, 59 (2), March/April 1999, 124–34.

Krashaar, Robert, and Barbara Beverly. "Library and Information Services for Productivity." *The Bookmark*, 48, Spring 1990, 167.

Krause, D.G. *Sun Tzu: The Art of War for Executives.* London: Nicholas Brealey, 1996.

Kress, Nancy, Darcy Del Bosque, and Tom Ipri. "User Failure to Find Known Library Items." *New Library World*, 112 (3/4), 2011, 150–170.

Kronus, Carol. "Patterns of adult library use: A regression and path analysis." *Adult Education*, 23, 1973, 115–31.

Lance, Keith Curry, Marcia J. Rodney, Nicolle O. Steffen, Suzanne Kaller, Rochelle Logan, Kristie M. Koontz, and Dean K. Jue, *Counting on results: New tools for outcome-based evaluation of public libraries.* Aurora, CO: Bibliographic Center for Research, 2002.

Lane, Lucious Page. "Monthly Report from Public Librarians Upon the Reading of Minors: A Suggestion." *Library Journal*, 23, August 1899, 479.

LaRue, James. "The Last One Standing." *Public Libraries*, 51 (1), January/February 2012, 28–32.

Lavoie, Brian. *The Top 25 U.S. Public Libraries' Collective Collection, as Represented in WorldCat.* Dublin, OH: OCLC, November 2011. Available at http://www.oclc.org/research/publications/library/2011/2011–02.pdf

LIANZA. *Manukau libraries: Trial of the V+LM Value Added Library methodology.* Trial Report. New Zealand: Library & Information Association of New Zealand, October 12, 2000.

Library Journal. *Ebook Penetration & Use in U.S. Public Libraries.* New York: Library Journal, 2011. Available for purchase at http://www.thedigitalshift.com/research/ebook-penetration/

Library Journal. *2011 Ebook Penetration & Use in U.S. Libraries Survey.* New York: Library Journal, October 12, 2011.

Library Journal. *2012 Survey of Ebook Usage in U.S. Public Libraries.* New York: Library Journal, 2012.

Line, Maurice. "What Do People Need of Libraries, and How Can We Find Out!" *Australian Academic & Research Libraries,* 27, June 1996, 79.

Lucas, Linda. "Reading Interests, Ife Interests, and Life-style." *Public Library Quarterly*, 3 (4), Winter 1982, 11–18.

Lugg, Rick, and Ruth Fischer. "Future Tense—Doing What's Obvious: Library Space and the Fat Smoker." *Against the Grain*, 21 (1), 2009, 75–76.

Lund, Leonard. *Locating corporate research and development facilities.* New York: The Conference Board, 1986.

Lynch, Mary Jo. "Using public libraries: What makes a difference?" *American Libraries*, 28 (10), November 1997, 64–65.

Lyne, Jack. "Quality-of-life factors dominate many facility location decisions." *Site Selection Handbook*, 33, August 1988.

MacEachern, Ruth. "Measuring the added value of library and information services: The New Zealand approach." *IFLA Journal* 27, (4), 2001, 232–37.

Madden, Michael. "Library User/Nonuser Lifestyles." *American Libraries*, 10 (2), February 1979, 78–81.

Magoolaghan, Michael. "Redesigning the Library Experience." *Bulletin of the American Society for Information Science & Technology*, 345 (1), October/November 2008, 41–43.

Marchant, Maurice. "What motivates adult use of public libraries?" *Library and Information Science Research*, 13, 1991, 201–35.

Markey, Karen. "The Online Catalog: Paradise Lost and Paradise Regained?" *D-Lib Magazine*, 13 (1/2), January/February 2007. Available at http://www.dlib.org/dlib/january07/markey/01markey.html

Markey, Karen, Schelle Simcox, and Eileen Fenton. "End-user understanding of Subject Headings in Library Catalogs." *Library Resources & Technical Services*, 43 (3), July 1999, 140–160.

Martell, Charles. "Theft and Its Effects on Our Neighborhood Libraries." *Public Library Quarterly*, 29 (1), 2010, 30–38.

Maryles, Daisey. "Behind the Bestsellers: Oprah's 'Opening." *Publishers Weekly*, 247 (35, 2000, 21.

Matthews, Joseph. "Customer Satisfaction: A New Perspective." *Public Libraries*, November/December 2008, 52–55.

Matthews, Joseph. *The Evaluation and Measurement of Library Services.* Westport, CT: Libraries Unlimited, 2007.

Matthews, Joseph. "What's the Return on ROI? The Benefits and Challenges of Calculating Your Library's Return on Investment." *Library Leadership & Management*, 25 (1), 2011, 1–14.

McClure, Charles, and John Carlo Bertot. *Public Library Use in Pennsylvania: Identifying Uses, Benefits, and Impacts—Final Report.* Harrisburg, PA: Pennsylvania Department of Education, Office of Commonwealth Libraries, 1998. ERIC ED419548

McClure, Charles R., Bruce T. Fraser, Timothy W. Nelson, and Jane B. Robbins. "Economic Benefits and Impacts from Public Libraries in the State of Florida: Final Report to State Library of Florida, Division of Library and Information Services." Tallahassee, FL: Information Use Management and Policy Institute, Florida State University, January 2001.

McCoppin, Robert. *Who's Killing the Dewey Decimal System?* Chicagotribune.com. February 18, 2011. Available at http://www.chicagotribune.com/news/ct-met-drop-dewey-20110218,0,7016754.story

McCarthy, Jerome. *Basic Marketing: A Managerial Approach.* Homewood, IL: Irwin, 1964.

McNeely, Cate. "The Library of the Future: A Status Report." Presentation at PLA 2000. Public Library Association, Eighth National Conference, March 30, 2000.

McNeely, Cate. "Organizational Creativity: How Richmond Public Library Used Creative Principles to Develop a Library for the Future." *PNLA Quarterly*, 65 (4), Summer 2001, 10,17.

McNulty, Robert. "The Economics of Amenity." *Meanjin*, 47 (4), Summer 1988, 615–24.

McQuaid, Heather, Aradhana Goel, and Mickey McManus. "When You Can't Talk to Customers: Using Storyboards and Narratives to Elicit Empathy for Users." *DPPI '03 Conference Proceedings*, June 23–26, 2003, 120–25.

Miele, T., and N. Welch. "Libraries as Information Centers for Economic Development." *Public Libraries*, 34 (1), January/February 1995, 18–22.

Mills, Terry. *The University of Illinois Film Center Collection Use Study.* Urbana, IL: Graduate School of Library and Information Science, 1982. ERIC ED227821.

Millsap, Gina. "Using Market Segmentation to Provide Better Public Library Services." *Marketing Library Services*, 25 (3), May-June 20112–4.

Mintzberg, Henry. "The Strategic Concept 1: Five Ps for Strategy." *California Management Review*, 30 (1), June 1987, 11–24.

Miringoff, Lee. *The Public Library: A National Survey.* Poughkeepsie, NY: The Marist College Institute for Public Opinion, 2003. A PowerPoint presentation of the poll's results is available at http://midhudson.org/funding/advocacy/Marist_Poll_2003.ppt

Mittermeyer, Diane. "Public Library Effectiveness: An Analysis of Values, Interests, and Benefits." *Canadian Journal of Information and Library Science*, 24 (4), December 1999, 1–32.

Monroe-Gulick, Amalia, and Lea Currie. "Using the WorldCat Collection Analysis Tool: Experiences From the University of Kansas Libraries." *Collection Management*, 36 (4), 2011, 203–216.

Morris, Anne, Margaret Hawkins, and John Sumsion. "Value of book borrowing from public libraries: User perceptions." *Journal of Librarianship and Information Science*, 33 (4), December 2001, 191–98.

Morville, Peter. *Ambient Findability.* Sebastopol, CA: O'Reilly, 2005, 55.

Nagy, Andrew. "Defining the Next-Generation Catalog." *Library Technology Reports*, October 2011, 11–15.

Nagy, Andrew. "The Impact of the Next-Generation Catalog." *Library Technology Reports*, October 2011, 18–20.

Nah, Fiona. "A Study on Tolerable Waiting Time: How Long Are Web Users Willing to Wait?" *Behaviour and Information Technology*, 23 (3), May-June 2004, 153–163.

Neiburger, Eli. "User-Generated Content." *Library Technology Reports*, November/December 2010, 13–24.

Newhouse, J.P., and A. J. Alexander. *An Economic Analysis of Public Library Services.* Santa Monica, CA: Rand Corporation, 1972.

Newman, Bobbi. "Should Libraries Get Out of the eBook Business?" *Librarian by Day blog,* March 7, 2012. Available at http://librarianbyday.net/2012/03/07/should-libraries-get-out-of-the-ebook-business/

Nisonger, Thomas. "A Review and Analysis of Library Availability Studies." *Library Resources & Technical Services*, 51 (1), January 2007, 30–49.

Noonan, D. *Contingent Valuation Studies in the Arts and Culture: An Annotated Bibliography.* Chicago: The Cultural Policy Center at the University of Chicago, 2002. Available at http://culturalpolicy.uchicago.edu/publications.html

Novotny, Eric. "I Don't Think I Click: A Protocol Analysis Study of Use of a Library Online Catalog in the Internet Age." *College & Research Libraries*, 65 (6), November 2004, 525–37.

NPD Group. *The 1996 Consumer Research Study on Book Purchasing.* Tarry-town, NY: Book Industry Study Group, 1996.

O'Brien, David, Urs Gasser, and John Palfrey. *E-Boobs in Libraries: A Briefing Document Developed in Preparation for a Workshop on E-Lending in Libraries.* Boston: The Berkman Center for Internet & Society at Harvard, Report No. 2012–15, 2012. Available at http://cyber.law.harvard.edu/publications/2012/ebooks_in_libraries

Ochola, John. "Use of Circulation Statistics and Interlibrary Loan Data in Collection Management." *Collection Management*, 27 (1), 2002, 1–13.

OCLC. *Online Catalogs: What Users Want and Librarians Want.* Dublin, OH: Online Computer Library Center, 2009.

OCLC. *Perceptions of Libraries and Information Resources.* Dublin, OH: Online Computer Library Center, 2005.

OCLC. *Perceptions of Libraries 2010: Context and Community.* Dublin, OH: Online Computer Library Center, 2010.

Oder, Norman. "In the Country of AnyThink." *Library Journal*, November 2010, 18–23.

OECD. *E books: Developments and Policy Considerations.* OECD Digital Economy Papers, No. 208. Paris: OECD Publishing, 2012. Available at http://dx.doi.org/10.1787/5k912zxg5svh-en

Olve, Nils-Goran, Jan Roy, and Magnus Wetter. *Performance Drivers: A Practical Guide to Using the Balanced Scorecard.* New York, Wiley, 1999.

O'Neill, Michael. "Effects of Signage and Floor Plan Configuration on Wayfinding Accuracy." *Environment and Behavior*, 23 (5), September 1991, 553–574.

Osborne, David, and Ted Gaebler. *Reinventing Government: How the Entrepreneurial Spirit is Transforming the Public Sector.* New York: Addison-Wesley, 1992.

Oserman, Steve, and Joan C. Durrance. "Providing Support For Job Seekers And Career Changers." *RQ*, 33 (3), Spring 1994, 322–25.

Ottensmann, John, Raymond Gnat, and Michael Geeson. "Similarities in Circulation Patterns Among Public Library Branches Serving Diverse Populations." *Library Quarterly*, 65 (1), January 1995, 89–118.

Palais, Elliot. *Availability Analysis Report.* SPEC Kit 71. Washington, DC: Association of Research Libraries, 1981.

Palmer, Susan. "The Effect Of Distance On Public Library Use: A Literature Survey." *Library Research*, 3, Winter 1981, 315–54.

Pankl, Robert R. "Marketing Practical Information." *Public Library Quarterly*, 20 (3), 2001, 41–60.

Patzer, Renee, and Thad Hartman. "Why Do We Dewey? Redesigning for the Customer Centered Experience." A presentation for Webjunction Kansas. Available at http://www.kslib.info/ce/why_do_we_dewey.PDF

Pearl, Nancy, and Sarah Statz Cords. *Now Read This III: A Guide to Mainstream Fiction.* Santa Barbara: Libraries Unlimited, 2010.

Peters, Tom. "Re-imagine!" New York: DK, 2003.

Pierce, Jennifer. "Picking the Flowers in the 'Fair Garden': The Circulation, Non-Circulation, and Disappearance of Young Adult Nonfiction Materials." *School Libraries Worldwide*, 9 (2), 2003, 62–72.

PinpointLogic. *COSLA: eBook Feasibility Study for Public Libraries.* Portland, OR: PinpointLogic, June 30, 2010.

Plohetski, Tony, and Andy Pierrotti. "Library Thefts Cost Austin More Than $1 Million in Five Years." *Statesman.com*, February 16, 2013. Available at http://www.statesman.com/news/news/local/library-thefts-cost-austin -more-than-1-million-in-/nWQ88/

Poister, Theodore, and Gregory Streib. "Performance Measurement in Municipal Government: Assessing the State of the Practice." *Public Administration Review*, 59 (4), July/August 1999, 325–35.

Porter, Michael. "What Is Strategy?" *Harvard Business Review*, 74 (6), November/December 1996, 61–78.

Powell, Ronald. "Library Use and Personality: The Relationship Locus of Control and Frequency of Use." *Library and Information Science Research,* 6, 1984, 179–90.

Powell, Ronald. *The Relationship Of Library User Studies To Performance Measures: A Review Of The Literature.* Occasional Paper Number 181. Champaign, IL: University of Illinois, Graduate School of Library and Information Science, 1988.

Prabha, Chandra, Lynn Connaway, Lawrence Olszewski, and Lillie Jenkins. "What is Enough? Satisficing Information Needs." *Journal of Documentation*, 63 (1), 2007, 74–89.

Purcell, Kristen. *Books or Nooks? How Americans' Reading Habits are Shifting in a Digitial World.* A presentation to the Ocean County Library Staff Development Day, May 18, 2012. Available at http://libraries.pewinternet .org/2012/05/18/books-or-nooks-how-americans-reading-habits-are-shift ing-in-a-digital-world/

Rainie, Lee. *Learning in the Digital Age*. Washington: Pew Internet Project, May 10, 2012. Available at http://pewinternet.org/Presentations/2012/May/Learning-in-the-digital-age.aspx

Rainie, Lee. *Networked Libraries Serving Networked Patrons*. Washington: Pew Internet Project, April 19, 2012. Available at http://pewinternet.org/Presentations/2012/Apr/Networked-libraries-serving-networked-patrons.aspx

Rashid, Haseeb. "Book Availability as a Performance Measure of a Library: An Analysis of the Effectiveness of a Health Sciences Library." *Journal of the American Society for Information Science*, 41 (7), 1990, 501–7.

Reidsma, Mathew. *You Library Website Stinks & It's Your Fault*. Presentation at the Library Technology Conference, St. Paul, Minnesota March 19, 2012. Available at http://matthew.reidsrow.com/articles/16

Rinkel, Gene, and Patrica McCandless. "Application of a Methodology Analyzing User Frustration." *College & Research Libraries*, 44, 1983, 29–37.

Roberts, Ken. *The Effects Of Non-Resident User Fees On Central Library Use*. Hamilton, ON: Hamilton Public Library, 1996.

Rodger, Eleanor Jo. "Value and Vision." *American Libraries*, 33 (10), November 2002, 50.

Rosen, Judith. "Classic Strategy, Classic Sales." *Publishers Weekly*, October 6, 2003, 16–18.

Ross, Catherine. *A Model of the Process of Choosing a Book for Pleasure*. A presentation at the American Public Library Association Spring Symposium, Chicago, March 25–27, 1999.

Ross, Catherine, and Mary Chelton. "Reader's Advisory: Matching Mood and Material." *Library Journal*, 126 (2), February 1, 2001, 52–55.

Samtani, Hiten. "Libraries Use iPads and Apps to Ramp Up Storytime, but Concerns Remain." *School Library Journal*, December 27, 2012,

Saracevic, Tefko, and Paul B. Kantor. "Studying the Value of Library and Information Services. Part I. Establishing a Theoretical Framework." *Journal of the American Society of Information Science*, 48 (6), 1997a, 527–542.

Saracevic, Tefko, and Paul B. Kantor. "Studying the Value of Library and Information Services. Part II. Methodology and Taxonomy." *Journal of the American Society of Information Science*, 48 (6), 1997b, 543–563.

Saricks, Joyce. *Readers' Advisory Service in the Public Library*. Chicago: American Library Association, 2005.

Saricks, Joyce. *The Readers Advisory Guide to Genre Fiction*. Chicago: American Library Association, 2001.

Sawyer, Rob. "The Economic and Job Creation Benefits of Ontario Public Libraries." *The Bottom Line*, 9 (4), 1996, 14–26.

Scales, Alice. "Examining What Older Adults Read and Watch on TV." *Educational Gerontology*, 22 (3), April/May 1996, 215–227.

Scheppke, Jim. "Who's Using the Public Library." *Library Journal*, 119, October 15, 1994, 35–37.

Schiemann, William, and John Lingle. *Bullseye! Hitting Your Strategic Targets Through High-Impact Measurement*. New York: Free Press, 1999, 61.

Schmenner, Roger W. *Making Business Location Decisions*. New York: Prentice Hall, 1982.

Schmidt, Aaron. "The User Experience: Catalog by Design." *Library Journal*, 138 (2), February 1, 2013, 19.

Schneider, Janet. *Floating Collections at Arapahoe Library District*. Englewood, CO: Araphoe Library District, July 2009.

Segal, Joseph. *The CREW Manual: A Unified System of Weeding, Inventory, and Collection-Building for Small and Medium-Sized Public Libraries*. Austin: Texas State Library, 1995.

Sendze, Monique. "The E-Book Experiment." *Public Libraries*, 51 (1), January/February 2012, 34–37.

Senge, Peter. *The Fifth Discipline*. New York: Doubleday, 1990, 206.

Senge, Peter. "The Practice of Innovation." *Leader to Leader*, 9, September 1998, 16–22.

Shaw, Debora, and Taemin Kim Park. "Comparing Users' Exchange Values with Library Costs in Academic and Public Libraries." *Proceedings of the ASIS Annual Meeting*, 31, 1994, 51–53.

Shearer, Kenneth. "Confusing What is Most Wanted with What is Most Used: A Crisis in Public Library Priorities Today." *Public Libraries*, 32, 1993, 193–97.

Sheffield Information Organization. *The Impact of Non-Fiction Lending from Public Libraries*. Sheffield, England: SINTO, 1999.

Skrzeszewski, Stan, and Maureen Cubberley. "Community-Based Economic Development and the Library—A Concept Paper." *Library Management*, 18 (7), 1997, 323–27.

Sloan, Paul. "A Guide to Open Innovation and Crowdsourcing: Advice from Leading Experts." London: Kogan Page, 2011.

Slote, Stanley. *Weeding Library Collections*. 4ᵗʰ Edition. Englewood, CO: Libraries Unlimited, 1997.

Smith, Adam. *An Inquiry into the Nature and Causes of the Walth of Nations*. New York: Modern Library, 1937.

Sone, Akio. "An Application of Discrete Choice Analysis to the Modeling of Public Library Use and Choice Behavior." *Library & Information Science Research*, 10, 1988, 35–55.

Speas, Linda. "Getting New Items into the Hands of Patrons: A Public Library Efficiency Evaluation." *Public Libraries*, 51 (6), November/December 2012, 24–31.

Spiller, David. "The Provision of Fiction for Public Libraries." *Journal of Librarianship*, 12 (4), October 1980, 238–65.

Stover, Jill. "Marketing is Code for Customer Service." *Library Marketing— Thinking Outside the Book blog*. January 5, 2006. Available at http://library marketing.blogspot.com/2006/01/marketing-is-code-for-customer-service .html

Sullivan, Michael. "Giving Them What They Want in Small Public Libraries." *Public Libraries*, 39 (3), May/June 2000, 148–55.

Sumsion, John, Margaret Hawkins, and Anne Morris. "Estimating the economic value of library benefits." *Performance Measurement and Metrics*, 4 (1), 2003, 13–27.

Surowiecki, James. *The Wisdom of Crowds*. New York: Anchor, 2005.

Swords, David (Ed.). "Patron-Driven Acquisitions: History and Best Practices." Boston, MA: De Gruyter Saur, 2011.

Tarulli, Laurel. *The Library Catalogue as Social Space*. Santa Barbara, CA: Libraries Unlimited, 2012.

Thompson, Arthur, Jr., and A. J. Strickland. *Crafting and Executing Strategy: Text and Readings*. New York: McGraw-Hill, 2001, 149.

Trueswell, Richard. "Some Behavioral Patterns of Library Users: The 80/20 Rule." *Wilson Library Bulletin*, 43 (5), January 1969, 458–61.

Tyler, David, Joyce Melvin, Xu Yang, Marylou Epp, Anita Kreps. "Effective Selectors? Interlibrary Loan Patrons as Monograph Purchasers: A Comparative Examination of Price and Circulation-Related Performance." *Journal of Interlibrary Loan, Document Delivery & Electronic Reserves*, 21 (1/2), January/June 2011, 57–90.

Tyler, David, Yang Xu, Joyce Melvin, Marylou Epp, and Anita Kreps. "Just How Right Are the Customers? An Analysis of the Relative Performance of Patron-Initiated Interlibrary Loan Monograph Purchases." *Collection Management*, 35, 2010, 162–179.

Ujiie, Joanne, and Stephen Krashen. "Are Prize-winning Books Popular Among Children? An Analysis of Public Library Circulation." *Knowledge Quest*, 34 (3), January/February 2006, 33–35.

Underhill, Paco. *Why We Buy: The Science of Shopping*. New York: Simon & Schuster, 1999.

Urban Libraries Council. *The Engaged Library: Chicago Stories of Community Building*. Evanston, IL: Urban Libraries Council, 2005.

U.S. Army Field Service Regulations, Operations. Washington, DC: U.S. Army, 2003.

U.S. News and World Report. More Americans Visit Their Public Library Today than They Did in 1978. Press Release. New York: U.S. News and World Report, December 2, 1995.

Usherwood, Bob, and R. Linley. "New library—New measures: A Social Audit of Public Libraries." *IFLA Journal*, 25 (2), 1999, 90–99.

Vaillancourt, R. J. *Bare Bones Young Adult Services: Tips For Public Library Generalists*. Chicago: American Library Association, 2002.

Vaughan, Liwen Qui, Jean Tague-Sutcliffe, and Pat Tripp. "The Value of the Library to Small Businesses." *RQ*, 36 (2), Winter 1996, 262–69.

Vaughn, Jason. "Web Scale Discovery: What and Why?" *Library Technology Reports*, 47 (1), January 2011, 5–11, 21.

Vaughn, Jason. "Investigations into Library Web-Scale Discovery Services." *Information Technology and Libraries*, March 2012, 32–82.

Vavrek, Bernard. "Is the American public library part of everyone's life?" *American Libraries*, 31 (1), 2000, 60–64.

Vinjamuri, David. "Why Public Libraries Matter: And How They Can Do More." *Forbes*, January 16, 2013. Available at http://www.forbes.com/sites/davidvinjamuri/2013/01/16/why-public-libraries-matter-and-how-they-can-do-more/

Voorbij, Henk. "The Value of LibraryThing Tags for Academic Libraries." *Online Information Review*, 36 (2), 2012, 196–217.

Wadley, Andrea, Judith Broady, and Tim Hayward. "An Evaluation of Current Public Library Service to the Full-Time Employed." *Library Management*, 18 (4), 1997a, 205–215.

Wadley, Andrea, Judith Broady, and Tim Hayward. "Marketing the Public Library service to the Full-Time Employed: Future Directions?" *Library Management*, 18 (5), 1997b, 253–263.

Waller, Vivienne. "Accessing the Collection of a Large Public Library: An Analysis of OPAC Use." *LIBRES,* 20 (1), March 2010, 1–27.

Way, Doug. "The Impact of Web-scale Discovery on the Use of a Library Collection." *Serials Review*, 36 (4), 2010, 217–220.

Webb, Jenn. "How Retailers Can Turn Showrooming into an Advantage." *Publishers Weekly*, June 25, 2012, 16.

Welch, Alicia, and Christine Donohue. "Awareness, Use, and Satisfaction with Public Libraries." *Public Libraries*, 33 (4), May/June 1994, 149–52.

Welker, Josh. "Counting on COUNTER." *Computers in Libraries*, November 2012, 6–11.

Wells, David. "What is a Library OPAC?" *The Electronic Library*, 25 (4), 2007, 386–394.

White, Hayley, Tim Wright, and Brenda Chawner. "Usability Evaluation of Library Online Catalogues." *Proceedings of the Seventh Australasian User Interface Conference, Hobart, Australia,* 2006, 50. Conferences in Research and Practice in Information Technology, Wayne Pickarski (Series Ed.). Available at http://crpit.com/confpapers/CRPITV50White.pdf

Willits, Harold, and Fern Willits. "Rural Reading Behavior and Library Usage: Findings from a Pennsylvania Survey." *Rural Libraries*, 11 (1), 1991, 25–37.

Wood, Judith, Julius Bremer, and Susan Saraidaridis. "Measurement of Service at a Public Library." *Public Library Quarterly*, 2, 1980, 49 57.

Yu, Liangzhi, and Ann O'Brien. "A Practical Typology of Adult Fiction Borrowing Based on Reading Habits." *Journal of Information Science*, 25 (1), January 1999, 35–49.

Zickuhr, Kathryn. *The Rise of e-Reading*. Washington, DC: Pew Research Center, October 12, 2012. Available at http://libraries.pewinternet.org/files/legacy-pdf/The%20rise%20of%20e-reading%204.5.12.pdf

Zickuhr, Kathryn, Lee Raine, Kristen Purcell. "Library Services in the Digital Age." Washington, DC: Pew Research Center, January 22, 2013. Available at http://libraries.pewinternet.org/2013/01/22/library-services/

Zickuhr, Kathryn, Lee Raine, Kristen Purcell, Mary Madden, and Joanna Brenner. *Libraries, Patrons, and e-Books*. Washington, DC: Pew Research Center, June 22, 2012. Available at http://libraries.pewinternet.org/2012/06/22/libraries-patrons-and-e-books/

Zweizig, Douglas. *Predicting Amount of Library Use: An Empirical Study of the Role of the Public Library in the Life of the Adult Public*. PhD Dissertation. Syracuse University, 1973.

Zweizig, Douglas, and Brenda Dervin. "Public Library Use, Users, and Uses: Advances in Knowledge of the Characteristics and Needs of the Adult Clientele of American Public Libraries." In *Advances in Librarianship*, 7, 1977, 232–57.

Index

About the Author

JOSEPH R. MATTHEWS is a consultant who has assisted numerous academic, public, and special libraries in a wide variety of projects. He was an instructor at the San Jose State University School of Library and Information Science. His recent published works include: *The Customer-Focused Library: Re-Inventing the Public Library From the Outside-In* (2009), *Evaluation and Measurement of Library Services* (2007), *Library Assessment in Higher Education* (2007, and *Measuring for Results: The Dimensions of Public Library Effectiveness* (2003) all with Libraries Unlimited.